NEITHER MALE
NOR FEMALE

This slim volume is a plea to those who continue to refuse a place for women in ministry to rethink their position, based on taking a more differentiated approach to Scripture, which, while affirming its authority, gives due attention to cultural and religious assumptions now rightly seen as outdated and inappropriate, and, in doing so, going beyond just the setting aside of requirements about women's attire to those deeming them best kept silent. An informed and impassioned read which invites discussion.
William Loader, Professor Emeritus of New Testament, Murdoch University

Noel Schultz in *Neither Male nor Female* exemplifies a somewhat lost art these days: the ability to be angry, sometimes deeply, yet to argue with respectful force, in order to advance a passionate case for re-thinking the role of women. He uses evidence from Scripture and elsewhere, and does not merely shout. And while clearly loyal to what drives church people to their commitment, he can't avert his gaze from the time-honoured prejudices within certain churches. This makes very good reading. You won't emerge quite the same after even short exposure.
Geraldine Doogue OAM, Broadcaster and Journalist

At what is potentially a pivotal time regarding the ordination of women in the Lutheran Church in Australia, this book retraces the steps of a journey from the unease of a young pastor at the teaching of his church regarding the status of women, through his exploration and research on the biblical texts used to support this position and his experience of working alongside women colleagues, to his quiet hope that women will soon be welcomed into the Church's ministry without the institution fracturing further. The book explores the texts that have been used to deny the full personhood of women using the language and methods of interpretation congruous for those who hold different views, while not accepting the framing of the discussion given by them. It is clear about the hermeneutical principles used and recalls the discussion of the Church at specific points in its history including the months following its most recent Synodical Convention. The book furthers a conversation that is yet to reach a resolution.
Dr Tanya Wittwer, Lecturer in Pastoral Theology, Adelaide College of Divinity / Flinders University, Brooklyn Park, South Australia

A clarion call to the Lutheran Church to restore women to their rightful place in the church. Lucid, thoughtful, determined, this book should be read by every church-goer still wrestling with the place of women in the church. Noel's clear, insightful thinking makes this book a must-read for all church goers, especially Lutherans in Australia and New Zealand who have not yet resolved the issue. Quo vadis, the church? Noel asks. And will women march with a church in which they cannot share in the leadership? Noel has been arguing for the full, equal place of women in the Australian church for almost half a century. This book is a powerful reminder that he has been right all along.

Dr Julia Baird, Author and Broadcaster

Neither Male nor Female is a much-needed tapestry of thoughts on the ongoing discussion regarding women's role and status within the Lutheran Church in Australia – an issue that continues to raise temperatures among people on both sides of the divide. The reflections offered here are derived from Noel C. Schultz's rich and personal experience within the church, and informed by Scripture, theology, history, and tradition. This book, the outcome of Schultz's passion rooted in the belief and the conviction that women are also called to serve the church, cannot be neglected. It stimulates our curiosity regarding the status of the debate on women's ordination within the LCA, as he urges fresh and renewed attention to the oft cited Scriptural texts and their dubious interpretations to deny women their rightful place in the church. By giving due consideration to the importance of Scripture and the hermeneutical principles employed, Schultz wrestles with these very same texts and distils from them valuable and illuminating insights into current questions of women's leadership. Above all, he offers a sound framework for debate and further creative thought and action by all and any committed to the equality of women and men in all aspects of church life.

Dr Monica Jyotsna Melanchthon
Associate Professor, Pilgrim Theological College, University of Divinity

Those who support the ordination of women will welcome Noel Schultz's detailed analysis of the texts that have been used within the Lutheran Church of Australia to exclude women from the ranks of the ordained ministry, namely 1 Corinthians 14:34-35 and 1 Timothy 2:11-14. I would also encourage those who favour the Church's current position to read the book carefully and weigh the evidence afresh. Noel's case for the inclusion of women in the ranks of the ordained ministry argument is based exclusively on the biblical text, against the repeated claim in some circles that advocates are motivated by social justice concerns, a feminist agenda, and disregard for the clear meaning of the text. In face of the entrenched notion that a supposed order of creation places women in a subordinate relationship to men, Noel concludes that the passages used in the debate have nothing to do with the ordination of women; instead, they deal with specific pastoral issues that had arisen at Corinth and Ephesus and impeded the free flow of the gospel. With an aching heart Noel prays that the baptismal unity of the faithful will soon find expression in the LCA as it works its painstaking way towards ensuring that women take their rightful place within the ordained ministry.

Rev Dr Peter Lockwood
Emeritus Lecturer, Australian Lutheran College

Noel Schultz's book began life as a thesis written forty years ago, to address the role of women in the Lutheran Church in Australia generally, and specifically the ordination of women. Dissatisfied with the theology present in the church in the 1970s and 80s that confined rather than liberated women in the church, Noel sought to gain a deeper, contextual reading of the biblical texts used in support of the status quo.
His thorough exegetical study of the key passages of scripture, which forms the demanding core of the book, repays effort. In its day Noel's thesis was a tract for its times. But for all readers this book signals a provocative question: have we fully understood the message and meaning of Jesus? Or have we allowed the truth of the Gospel to be imprisoned in presuppositions that rob it of the deeper meaning conveyed by the Word made flesh himself?

The Rev Dr John Smith
Uniting Church Minister (retired)

Neither Male nor Female

THE BIBLE
WOMEN & THE MINISTRY
OF THE CHURCH

NOEL C. SCHULTZ

COVENTRY
PRESS

Published in Australia by
Coventry Press
33 Scoresby Road
Bayswater VIC 3153

ISBN 9780648861270

Copyright © Noel C. Schultz 2020

All rights reserved. Other than for the purposes and subject to the conditions prescribed under the *Copyright Act*, no part of this publication may be reproduced, stored in a retrieval system, or transmitted in any form or by any means, electronic, mechanical, photocopying, recording or otherwise, without the prior permission of the publisher.

Scripture quotations are from the *New Revised Standard Version Bible* © 1989, Division of Christian Education of the National Council of the Churches of Christ in the United States of America. Used by permission. All rights reserved.

Catalogue-in-Publication entry is available from the
National Library of Australia http://catologue.nla.gov.au

Cover design by Ian James – www.jgd.com.au
Text design by Coventry Press
Set in Fontin 11.5 pt

Printed in Australia

Table of Contents

Acknowledgments v
Preface vii
Introduction x
Chapter 1 Historical and Personal Background 1
  How Ministry is Understood 2
  Ministry in Today's Society 4
  Historical Setting: The Theses of Agreement 5
  My Search Begins 7
  The Way Forward 11
Chapter 2 Neither Male nor Female *Galatians 3:26-29* .. 14
  Introducing A Seeming Conflict 15
  A Foundational Declaration to a People Divided 16
  Overturning a World View 20
    Neither Jew nor Greek 21
    Neither Slave nor Free 24
    Neither Male nor Female 27
  Cultural and Religious Background 29
  A Radical Message 31
  Paul Under Scrutiny 32
  Females in Ministry in New Testament Times 35
  Summary Conclusion 41

Chapter 3 The Silence Expected of Wives in the
            Worship at Corinth 42
The Corinthian Setting 43
Dealing with the Disorder 44
Not Parallel Statements 46
The Weight of the Cultural Context 47
No Parallel to Women in Ministry Today 48
Chapter 4 The Teaching Forbidden to Wives
            1 Timothy 2:8-15 52
The Authorship of the Pastorals 55
Background and Destination of 1 Timothy 56
   Relationship to 1 Corinthians 14:33-35 57
   What is the Timothy Passage Saying in Its Context? 58
   The Crucial Verses 60
Combating False Teachers 61
How 'Teaching' is Described 63
   A Key Word 66
The Serious Problem in the Church 68
   How Valid are the Reasons for Not Teaching? 71
First Century Jewish Influences 74
Need to Review and Discard 75
Chapter 5 Creation and Fall Narratives
            Genesis 1:26-28; 2:4-24; 3:1-21 79
The Creation Story in Genesis 1 81
The Creation Story in Genesis 2 82
The Fall into Sin and the Curse – Genesis 3:1-21 .. 87
   Male Dominance over Females 89
Chapter 6 Hermeneutical Presuppositions 93
Then and There: Here and Now 96
Specific Instructions for Specific Situations 97

Context and Culture – of Paramount Consideration .. 101
In Summary 104
Chapter 7 *Quo Vadis*, LCA? 106
Close Ties with Overseas Churches 107
The Decision to Exclude Women 108
Changes in Teaching and Practice 111
Churches Benefit from Women in Public Ministry ... 112
Why Does the LCA Persist in Excluding Women? 113
Theses of Agreement 115
Constitution, By-laws and Synodical Procedures 116
What the LCA Continues to Teach and Practise 119
Post 2018 Convention 122
So, *Quo Vadis*, LCA/NZ? 126
End notes 130
Selected Bibliography 146

Acknowledgments

SOME VERY SPECIAL PEOPLE made an important contribution to the publishing of this book – John Smith, our former minister and treasured friend, who suggested the name of a possible publisher; Hugh McGinlay, of Coventry Press, whose advice, support and courage saw the book published; and Lyndal Fuller, who efficiently and cheerfully located the source of important references from LCA synods and official reports. Special thanks to William Loader, Peter Lockwood and Tanya Wittwer for the valued suggestions they provided and for putting me in touch with helpful recent literature.

The writing of the DMin thesis, 'Neither Male nor Female – Towards a Theology and Practice of Equality of the Sexes in the Lutheran Church of Australia', a starting point for much of this book, resulted from being selected by the LCA to accept a scholarship offered by the Evangelical Lutheran Church of America to participate in the Ministry in Pastoral Care in Social Change program offered at Luther-North-Western Theological Seminary, St Paul, Minnesota, during the academic year 1978-79. For the subsequent writing of the thesis I was greatly encouraged and assisted by American friends, and especially by Norman Bakken, and by Australian colleagues, Herman Pech and Victor Pfitzner. The person who made by far the greatest contribution to the writing both of the thesis and the present book decades later, has been my wife, Cynthia. In the midst of completing her PhD, she willingly became involved in the early planning for my thesis during Minnesota's coldest winter on record and, on our return to a much warmer Brisbane, provided encouragement and editorial expertise to ensure its completion.

Now, many years later, for the writing of this book, I am again grateful for the important contribution Cynthia has made to ensure the contents met the same standards she maintained in her own books and in the university journal she edited. After sixty-five years of marriage, there is not much on which we disagree – except on occasions on the use of 'which' or 'that'. Our children Julianne, Cindy and Andrew, richly endowed with a deep concern for social justice and a search for truth, have shared in the challenges, hopes and achievements of our profoundly satisfying life. Their loving participation and life-long involvement in their parents' story have added a vital dimension to the life for which we have continued to be profoundly grateful. Prior to the threatened outbreak of Covid-19 in Melbourne's northern suburbs, Cindy and husband Alistair ensured that Cynthia and I were relocated to a much safer environment – their home in Central Victoria. It was from this loving environment that the final stages of the book were completed. Their contribution to the writing of this book included significant technical support. The insights that Julianne provided from her writing and publishing experience, and Andrew's ongoing moral support, are acknowledged with profound gratitude.

Preface

AS A TEENAGER GROWING UP in the Queensland district of the still young Lutheran Church of Australia (LCA) in the early 1970s, I remember being aware even then that Noel Schultz's voice was a prophetic one. This is borne out by what he is publishing here, which is in essence the research he conducted in that decade during his DMin studies at an Evangelical Lutheran Church in America (ELCA) seminary in Minnesota. What he wrote then remains as fresh and relevant today to the Australian and New Zealand Lutheran context. It demonstrates both how forward-thinking he was at the time and how little has changed in the debates within Australasian Lutheranism about gender and the pastoral office.

This small book is timely as a reminder of a missional focus that is often missing from this debate and of the implications of that missional aspect for the LCA/NZ's future. In the wake of the 2018 General Convention of Synod the depth of the division within the church that centres on this issue has risen to the surface and is now exposed to the public eye. Few Australasian Lutherans can remain unaware that, as the General Bishop has himself acknowledged, we are a church in schism. What remains less well articulated is the gap between the missional outlook and witness of our Lutheran schools and this intractable dispute over ministry and gender. I and my siblings, together with Noel's and Cynthia's children, attended St Peters Lutheran College at Indooroopilly, Brisbane, in the 70s. There we learnt daily in chapel about God's unbounded grace, and in our classes that gender was no barrier to achievement. In both families, as with so many other students of that school, we have achieved extraordinary heights in our careers because of that foundation.

The pain of graduates of our Lutheran schools as a result of the church's inability to achieve consensus and clear direction on this issue is real and the consequences damaging. With one hand, the church speaks grace and equality in Christ to the students educated in its schools; with the other, it tells the graduates of those schools who are called by the Spirit to serve that the same God who frees them to be who they are then limits the ministry options to which, through that same Spirit, he has called them. Some who are set free in Christ, it says, are more special than others.

After the 2018 General Convention, one St Peters graduate shared that, having been brought to the faith in school and assured of her worth in God's eyes, she now felt compelled to leave a church that was telling her that she is, despite all her achievements in a demanding male-dominated secular profession, in that same God's eyes by virtue of her gender second-rate.

Preface

This conflicting message is one that hinders the message of hope that Christ brought and continues to bring to the world. Noel's engagement with these long-contested scriptural passages brings to the forefront awareness of that divine ungendered call – to ministry and mission.

Professor Wendy Mayer
Fellow of the Australian Academy of the Humanities
(Head, Religion Section)
Associate Dean for Research, Australian Lutheran College
Dean of Research Strategy, University of Divinity.

Introduction

FROM THE MIDDLE OF THE LAST CENTURY in churches of all denominations – Reformed, Protestant, Catholic, Orthodox – clergy, academics, laymen and laywomen began to raise questions about the role and status of women in their churches. For generations, women in their churches had been mothers and child-raisers, teachers in Sunday schools and church schools, church cleaners and flower arrangers, choristers and organists, morning tea and lunch providers, but not elders, council members, conference delegates, voting members, and certainly not preachers nor celebrants! As women in the community began to take on more leadership roles in all walks of life, some women and men began to ask why not also in the church? For decades, reasons were advanced on the basis of tradition and Scripture that women are not entitled to have the same positions or offices that men had occupied since time immemorial.

The outcome of prolonged debates and conferences in some Christian churches was an acceptance that women and not just men could be persons with authority, decision-makers, priests and even bishops. But this change of standing did not come about easily. For some the movement towards gender equality was reluctantly recognised in theory, but no change took place in church policy. Women were still excluded from congregational and national church councils, and from the pulpit. For some, debates dragged on for generations, and though women were reluctantly allowed to serve in positions of some authority in their local congregations, they were still considered disqualified from the office of the public ministry. Those who stubbornly refused to accept female ministers or priests argued that Christ's disciples were male, women were not priests or ministers for more than a thousand years of church history, and furthermore, they were declared to be disqualified in the Scriptures of the New Testament.

From the mid-20th Century, right up to the present time, literature, books, and treatises have poured out of universities, theological faculties, religious and secular printing houses denouncing or proclaiming women's new standing and role in the church. For some denominations, the issue is still not resolved. In some branches of the same religious family what is accepted as one of the most important and positive actions for generations is condemned, just as vigorously, by others as an aberration and a repudiation of Scripture and tradition. There are those who have experienced church life under both regimes.

Large parts of the exegetical studies that constitute major sections of this book were written four decades ago. Over the intervening years, I have become even more convinced of the correctness of the approach shown in these studies. There is nothing of substance that I would want to change, but some important additions have been made. During the years that have transpired, I have had the privilege of observing first-hand how my understanding of these passages are a lived-out reality in the Evangelical Lutheran Church in the United States (ELCA) and the Uniting Church in Australia (UCA). In these Churches, women do become bishops, moderators, presidents of theological seminaries as well as ministers and missionaries.

Whilst the ELCA, the UCA and the Lutheran Church in Australia (LCA) share a common understanding of what are the privileges, tasks and responsibilities of ministers, in the LCA at least half its membership is disqualified from sharing in the church's public ministry because of their gender. Among the world-wide Lutheran churches whose membership numbers some 70 million, all except the LCA, the Lutheran Church – Missouri Synod, and a few others, ordain women and have done so for decades.

What is being attempted in the following pages is to raise serious questions about the ways in which the LCA, both in its historical practices, and even at the time of writing, has failed to act in accordance with the realities of male/female equality by its decisions not to ordain women into the ministry of the church. Surely this is one of the most basic expressions of the gospel's intent for our day. Is it not a contradiction to preach about God's acceptance of both men and women into his family for Christ's sake, and at the same time to insist on practices that deny women an equal standing with men in the church? In the concrete realities of life in the Lutheran Church in Australia and New Zealand, no woman, no matter how well-qualified and dedicated, can be called into the public ministry of preaching and teaching the Word and administering the sacraments. It has continued to maintain that women must be excluded from the church's ministry because it claims that the Scriptures insist on this action. In the following pages, the claim that Scriptures teach that women cannot be ordained ministers in the church will be carefully analysed and shown to be a serious misapplication of the passages in question.

Until quite recent times, women were denied the opportunity of serving in their congregations as elders, lay readers, or major office bearers; in some congregations, women were not permitted to read the gospel in public worship, could gather around the Lord's Table only after the men had communed, could not vote at business meetings of the congregation and could not represent their congregations at state and national conventions. How have such practices in the past, and the current refusal to ordain women into the ministry of the church, borne or bear witness to the redemptive work of Christ on behalf of women and men? Even on the basis of common justice, such practices need to be questioned and rejected. The task ahead is to examine the thinking behind such practices, the theological arguments used to justify these rules, and the misuse of Scripture in order to provide justification for these practices (some of which are now regarded with embarrassment).

If the reader is curious to know why I am no longer a minister in the Lutheran Church in Australia, a word of explanation is in place. In 1981, after a ten year ministry in St Andrews Lutheran Church, which saw the successful uniting of two central city congregations in Brisbane and the opening of the contemporary church on Wickham Terrace, I was ready to continue my ministry in another city and was offered the position of Director of Pastoral Care and Community Education at a large, central city UCA church in Melbourne. I applied for leave of absence from the Lutheran Church to undertake this challenging position. The Lutheran Church in Queensland agreed to this request, but the national body refused, claiming that to celebrate Holy Communion in this church would be contrary to Lutheran practice, even though the Melbourne church insisted that I could celebrate Holy Communion using Lutheran liturgical format. (Incidentally, a few years later the LCA and the UCA came to a shared understanding of Holy Communion liturgy.) Consequently, I resigned from the Lutheran Church in order to accept the Melbourne church's offer and was readily received into the ministry of the Uniting Church.

My final word is an expression of profound gratitude that the Lord of the church has ransomed me at such a great cost and in his wisdom and grace has called me to exercise ministry in the church. I am also grateful that over the years, and in particular as a consequence of these studies, I have developed a deep love and a growing understanding of the New Testament Scriptures on which the church of every age, guided by the Holy Spirit, is dependent for its understanding of the revelation disclosed through Jesus Christ.

Noel C. Schultz
June 2020

Chapter 1

Historical and Personal Background

MY INTEREST IS LONG-STANDING IN an area of Scripture and church practice that has been and continues to be a cause of disquiet and serious unrest not just for me, but also for large sections of church communities. What had been a disturbing question for some time is how could any Christian church persist in a teaching and a practice which suggested that it is God's will for all time that more than half the world's population should be subordinate to the remainder? In other words, was it Christian theology that women ontologically, by virtue of their gender, are intrinsically subordinate to men in general, and, therefore, because of the 'created order of things', must take a subordinate or secondary role to men in the church?

Undoubtedly, a great many people, outside the church, but within the church as well, would quickly and rightly dismiss such questions as ridiculous anachronisms. These questions raise serious implications also for the Lutheran Church of Australia (LCA), within which I had been ordained. Had not my church, therefore, in its past teachings and practices, and even in its current rejection of women's ordination, been party to creating this false and offensive image?

Before proceeding to an examination of the historical basis to these questions, it is important to summarise my understanding of ministry, because ministry in the church is what this book is primarily about.

How Ministry is Understood

Ministry is understood primarily as service, in accordance with Christ's very explicit instructions in this regard.[1] Ministry is undertaken in his name, in the power of the Spirit, with the gifts supplied by the Spirit, on behalf of people, for the edifying of the church.[2] The chief focus of ministry is on the death and resurrection of Christ, and the life, freedom and hope this means for people the Spirit leads to faith.[3]

My understanding of ministry incorporates the following convictions:

i. God has called me to take a part in making known the gospel of Jesus Christ through preaching, teaching, administering the sacraments, absolving and counselling.
ii. The church has called me to exercise this ministry in specific places at different times.
iii. The Spirit has enabled and equipped me for ministry with gifts to be used for the benefit of others.
iv. The model which has particular appeal to me is the minister as the servant of Christ.

v. The minister has both a prophetic role (preaching, proclaiming) and a priestly role (counselling, encouraging, supporting).[4]

vi. The gospel which gives substance and purpose to the ministry is essentially a liberating message. In our time, people are troubled by feelings of alienation, anxiety, loneliness and worthlessness. Divisions growing out of racial, economic, ideological and gender differences run deep in our society. The ministry of Word and sacrament has the privilege and challenge of presenting the gospel in all its richness and saving power to people in ways that are most meaningful and relevant in today's world.

vii. Faithfulness to the gospel and the biblical record may result in the ministry challenging concepts and traditions, which though hallowed through age and long usage, may be seen in our day to be at variance with the truth of the gospel. It is therefore incumbent on the ministry to recognise that there are social implications of the gospel and to ensure that the liberating message of the gospel is to be applied to the social and institutional realities of present-day life.[5]

Faithfulness to the gospel demands a speaking out against anything that is a denial of the here and now consequences of Christ's redemptive work on behalf of male and female. Those called into the office of ministry in the church ought to be 'generators of vision among God's people' and ready to disturb the *status quo* when practices and decisions threaten the truth of the gospel.[6]

Ministry in Today's Society

In a time when gender equality is a much prized reality in Australia, New Zealand, the United States and many other parts of world, to treat women as somehow inherently unsuited because of their gender from being called into the ministry of the church is not a message or practice that proclaims the freedom, hope and unity of the gospel. Instead it is an action that insists on the maintenance of outmoded social norms where women were widely treated as subordinate to men, and therefore disqualified from exercising the same position of leadership and ministry in the church as men.

What would be an appropriate response and testimony to the 'creative power of the gospel' would be to encourage women to use the gifts of the Spirit entrusted to them for all manner of service and leadership in the local church and national body, and certainly to invite those who feel called by God to seek ordination to the ministry of Word and sacrament in their church.[7] Both the role and the status of women have changed dramatically over the past hundred years. Women's role in western society a hundred years ago was probably closer to that which prevailed in the first century of the Christian era than that which is common in our time. Patriarchal, androcentric attitudes, for which there is no lack of evidence in the history of Christianity, are rightly offensive to both men and women today.

Historical Setting: The Theses of Agreement

In 1955, the first year of my ministry in New Zealand, serious questions were being raised in some congregations concerning the status of women in the church. The previous year, the much loved President of the then Evangelical Lutheran Church of Australia, the Reverend Dr Clemens Hoopmann, had presented a paper at the convention of the Evangelical Lutheran Conference of New Zealand, in which he claimed that 'according to the order of creation a more subordinate position has been given to woman than to man'.[8] He argued that 'this subjection is a biblical principle referred to in many passages of Holy Writ, beginning with Genesis 3:16'. He maintained that 1 Corinthians 14:34-35 and 1 Timothy 2:11-14 prohibit 'speaking and teaching by women in public Christian assembly', and that 'this broad and permanent principle prohibits the casting of votes by women on equal terms with men' at congregational meetings.[9] Dr Hoopmann's paper was an important contribution in an area of growing concern at the time, not only in the scattered congregations in New Zealand, but also in the Lutheran churches 'across the ditch' in Australia. Quite clearly, this church leader's statements were an expression of the view held by theologians and leaders of the Lutheran Church in Australia.

A few years earlier, a statement on the two Lutheran churches' understanding of ministry was agreed to by both branches of the divided Lutheran Church in Australia and incorporated into the 'Theses of Agreement' which was a basis in 1966 for the formation of the Lutheran Church in Australia (LCA). In 'VI: Theses on the Office of the Ministry', the final paragraph reads:

> Though women prophets were used by the Spirit of God in the Old and as well as in the New Testament, 1 Corinthians 14:34-35 and 1 Timothy 2:11-14 prohibit a woman from being called into the office of the public ministry for the proclamation of the Word and the administration of the Sacraments. This apostolic rule is binding on all Christendom; hereby her rights as a member of the spiritual priesthood are in no wise impaired.[10]

The reason the final statement of Theses VI, which otherwise presented the historic Lutheran understanding of ministry, should rule out the possibility of women being ordained in the new church soon to be established, was the fear, expressed by lecturers at the seminary where I was a student, that some Lutheran churches in Europe were about to or already had ordained women in their church's ministry. The final paragraph was intended to prevent such 'an aberration' occurring in the church 'down under'. Even made was the bombastic claim that 'This apostolic rule is binding on all Christendom'!

Quite clearly, Dr Hoopmann's statement and the final paragraph of the 'Theses on the Office of the Ministry' need to be seen in the historical setting of seventy years ago in Australian Lutheran communities where women were regarded as subordinate to men. If they were not permitted to vote at business meetings of the congregation and could not hold any major office in the local congregation, and were not entitled to represent their congregations at state and federal conventions, perish the scandalous and heretical thought that they might become pastors and teach men! It is doubtful that any woman in the '50s from a local Australian

Lutheran church would have ever dreamed of holding such a prominent and authoritative position as a pastor. In the predominantly rural communities in which the Lutheran church was strongly represented, equality of the sexes was not a topic of lively conversation. Though women in that era had played a minor, though vital, part in the war just concluded, and though a very small number were prominent in the political sphere, there was relatively little agitation for gender equality in the community, and certainly not in the male dominated Lutheran church. Consequently, when the theologians of the two Lutheran synods decreed the inability of women to hold the office of pastor, they did not have to experience the sort of opposition and alarm such a decree receives today when their successors persist in making such a claim.

Nevertheless, there were a few voices raised in protest in local congregations in New Zealand, and a few pastors who felt that Dr Hoopmann's statement and the Theses of Agreement needed to be questioned. My view at the time was that it was an inadequate treatment of significant passages, especially 1 Corinthians 14:34-35, 1 Timothy 2:11-14 and Genesis 3:16. In an attempt to have a more thorough study of the passages undertaken, the pastors of the New Zealand Lutheran Church asked the Faculty of Concordia Seminary in Adelaide (where most of the pastors working in New Zealand had been trained) to prepare an exegetical study of the New Testament passages in question. I have no record of the outcome of this request.

My Search Begins

I was not prepared to simply accept that the way passages of Scripture had been interpreted for generations in the LCA to maintain women's subordination to men and their exclusion from the office of ministry were binding on members of the church in today's world. I attempted on several occasions to grapple with the exegetical and hermeneutical challenges involved in the study of New Testament passages dealing with the status and role of women in the church and society at large; but such searching tended to raise more questions than it answered. Pressures of parish responsibilities and ongoing substantial involvement in synodical and community work provided a convenient excuse not to become more deeply involved. There the matter would have probably remained, but for the fact that I was able, thanks to a scholarship provided by the Evangelical Lutheran Church in America, to spend the academic year, 1978-79, enrolled in a Ministry in Pastoral Care program sponsored by the Minnesota Consortium of Theological Seminaries. The program's director was Dr William Hulme. During a seminar on Continuing Education, Dr Henry Gustafson of United Theological Seminary, responded warmly to the concern I expressed about Paul's statement on women. He encouraged me to make this an area for on-going study. During the long, cold and dreary winter months of that year in St Paul, Minnesota, I read extensively in the area, and under the excellent guidance of Dr Donald Juel of Luther Theological Seminary, prepared a paper entitled 'Neither Male nor Female and the Corinthian Situation'.

It was not my intention at the time to take the matter any further, since I had arrived at personally satisfactory answers to the questions that had concerned me throughout my ministry. But events then transpired that compelled me – almost against my will – to develop this matter further into a thesis project. It had been my intention to undertake a thesis project in the other area of special interest in my ministry – the family. Certainly, this would have been a much 'safer' area to work in, and had I been concerned about my status in the LCA, I would have avoided the controversial area of women's role and status in the church. Yet knowing in advance the sort of pressure that could be expected, I decided to pursue the study further for the following reasons:

1. I was appalled that the August 1978 Convention of the LCA could not agree to grant women the right to be delegates of their congregations at synodical conventions.[11]
2. I considered it a serious omission for this church not to disown and reject the 1966 theological statement of the Faculties of Concordia Seminary and Immanuel Seminary: '1. In Christ man and woman have equal standing, Mark 12:25 and parallels, Galatians 3:28, but there is a difference between man and woman by virtue of the fact of creation, 1 Corinthians 11:7-10; 1 Timothy 2:13; Genesis 2:1ff, by which a subordinate position has been given to women. A further reason is the role played by woman at the fall, Genesis 3:1ff; 1 Timothy 2:14. This subordination shows itself as far as the individual woman is concerned in the marriage relation, Genesis 3:16.2. This difference between man and woman, traceable back to creation and the fall is not set aside in the Christian church as it exists on earth, where it is subject to all the ordinances of creation: 1 Corinthians 11:3,10; Ephesians 5:21f; Colossians 33:18; 1 Peter 3:5ff.'[12]
3. I was convinced that the resolution adopted by the 1968 Convention of the General Synod in reluctantly giving women a vote at congregational meetings was in serious error, because it insisted that when women are given the right to discuss and vote in congregations, 'the principle that in our congregations the woman is in subjection to

the man be safeguarded by recognising the right of the men to reserve the final decision on any matter to a male vote whenever the men desire to invoke this right'.[13]
4. I was aware in undertaking this study that the insights of the social sciences and history should not be disparaged, especially when they compel us to come to terms with our presuppositions. It may not be possible to rid oneself completely of sexual or other bias in seeking to understand a given passage of Scripture. I would not be so bold or foolish to claim that in undertaking this study I would succeed in letting the Scriptures speak for themselves, for that would be impossible. The problem is confounded by the fact that not only does the reader tend to read back into Scripture their own cultural orientation over against women's role and status, but also by the fact that the writers of Scripture wrote from a particular historical, cultural, social and religious background. Accordingly, the assumptions and prejudices of their culture could not help but be reflected both in what the writer wrote and what they did not write. Just as the eternal Word became one of us at a precise period in history and lived out his life, sharing in the cultural and religious ethos of his day, so the written Word of the New Testament came to us out of the Jewish cultural and historical background of the first century C.E., very different from our own. I was determined not to allow my presuppositions impinge upon the historical record, especially the utterly amazing revelation given to us concerning God's intervention in human history in the life of Jesus Christ.
5. It was my ardent hope, in proceeding with the writing of the DMin thesis, entitled 'Neither Male nor Female:

Towards a theology and practice of sexual equality in the Lutheran Church of Australia', that the studies it embraced might provide a stimulus for at least some sections of the Lutheran Church of Australia to move away from a literalistic interpretation of several Scripture passages whilst maintaining the *sola scriptura* principle so much valued by this church.[14] To this end, 30 pastors of the LCA agreed to read and respond to the material I was sending them, namely, i) The exegetical studies (Galatians 3:26-29; the Creation and Fall narratives; 1 Corinthians 11:2-16 and 14:34-35; Ephesians 5:21-33; 1 Timothy 2:8-15); ii) Summary of hermeneutical principles employed; iii) Some practical implications for the life and practice of the LCA, and iv) A response guide.

6. The further my research and writing proceeded, the stronger became my distress that for decades this church had maintained the notion of women's subordination to men and their consequent exclusion from roles and functions of leadership in the church.

The Way Forward

Surely the church must spell out the implications of the gospel to its membership so as to bring about change in practices and attitudes where this is necessary. In so doing, such a church is giving a clearer witness to that gospel than the church which prefers the *status quo*. Those entrusted with the public proclamation of the gospel and the administration of the sacraments have a special responsibility to provide leadership so that a clear, unambiguous witness is given to the gospel.[15] This is a very urgent need in our day, especially since the secular world is far ahead of the church in ensuring that gender equality is a reality. In fact, if the church regards more than half of its membership as somehow unacceptable for the ministry because of their gender, it stands condemned by the secular world for its inconsistency, even hypocrisy, because its proclamation of the gospel which speaks of acceptance, unity and equality is not lived out in the reality of its own membership.

Changes to deeply entrenched social and cultural conditions do not come about without conflict and prolonged struggle. For sixty years, Lutherans in Australia and New Zealand have debated the issue of women's role and status in their church. Similar debates have been taking place also among Anglicans, Presbyterians, Baptists, and Lutherans in Sweden, the United States, Canada, England and Germany. For a church that places great importance on the authority of the Scriptures to determine all matters of faith and practice, there is bound to be a prolonged struggle and sharp division when its traditional understanding of some long-held practice is seriously questioned. Tension there will always be when the centrality of the gospel (with all its implications for contemporary people) is applied in a church environment where there has been a fundamentalist tendency in its application of Scripture. The tension continues to be a distressing reality in the LCA today.[16]

Critics will be (and have been) quick to point out that by raising questions about the interpretation and application of certain biblical passages in reference to the role of women in the church, the authority of the Scriptures is being questioned. In subsequent chapters, readers will have to determine for themselves whether I have been faithful both to the gospel and to the Scriptures as the church's authoritative guide and rule.[17] To assist in that process, the

Historical and Personal Background

following chapters address the current issues of concern in a study of significant passages of Scripture from the Old and New Testaments.

Chapter 2

Neither Male nor Female
Galatians 3:26-29

IN ANY DISCUSSION ON THE ROLE AND STATUS of women in the church, this passage from Galatians is invariably one of the first quoted.[18] But there is a sharp difference in the way users of this passage understand its applicability. Accordingly, the question of major concern in respect to Galatians 3:26-29 may be stated this way: Is Paul describing how it is for Jew and Greek, slave and free, male and female *coram deo*, that is, only in their relationship with God, or is he going further and declaring that the relationships such people have with their God have far-reaching implications also in the here and now of their social relationships in church and society?

It is my contention that the apostle Paul is doing more than merely describing the spiritual relationship assorted believers have with God through faith in Jesus Christ; he is also outlining in dramatic terms the broader relationships resulting from the unity which is given us through baptism. This unity has a crucial impact on racial, religious, social and gender attitudes and behaviours.

There are two reasons, in addition to the obvious meaning of the text itself, which strongly support this contention. In the first place, this passage is a major theological statement, an integral part of the gospel, and is thus deserving of primacy in a consideration of related passages of Scripture.

The second reason for my contention that this passage goes beyond the believer's relationship with God is the explicit teaching and practice of Paul himself in regard to some of the implications.

Introducing A Seeming Conflict

Before developing these arguments further, attention should be drawn to the reality confronting the New Testament reader when some passages are placed side by side:

> *Galatians 3:25-28* But now that faith has come, we are no longer subject to a disciplinarian, for in Christ Jesus you are all the children of God through faith. As many of you as were baptised into Christ have clothed yourselves with Christ. There is no longer Jew or Greek, there is no longer slave or free, there is no longer male and female; for all of you are one in Christ Jesus.
>
> *Colossians 3:18* Wives, be subject to your husbands, as is fitting in the Lord.
>
> *1 Corinthians 14:34* As in all the churches of the saints, women should keep silent in the churches. For they are not permitted to speak, but should be subordinate.
>
> *1 Timothy 2:12* I permit no woman to teach or to have authority over a man; she is to keep silent.

In the face of seemingly explicit statements demanding of women a much more restricted role than that granted to men, it is to be expected that the Bible reader senses a conflict if 'there is no longer male or female' implies equality of the sexes in church and society. Now that conflict or contradiction will of course disappear if the Galatian passage is restricted in its application to women's status before God. Though it is possible that a Bible student might understand the Galatian text as a purely spiritual relationship, even if they had never heard of Colossians 3:18, 1 Corinthians 14:35 and 1 Timothy 2:14, it is more likely that such texts would be a powerful influence in arriving at such a conclusion. The exegete can easily find their mind made up concerning Galatians 3:26-29 before they even look at it, because of what they think is said elsewhere concerning woman's subordinate role in life. There is special value, therefore, in beginning a study of biblical passages with Galatians, especially if the passage is allowed to speak for itself and presuppositions from elsewhere are not allowed to intrude on the text.

A Foundational Declaration to a People Divided

The underlying principle to which I hold is that some portions of Scripture are of greater normative value for the church than others. Those passages of Scripture, which deal with God's revelation of the saving plans and redemptive activity concerning Jesus Christ, are of ultimate importance for the church in every age. Where some principle or theological insight is grounded in the gospel revelation, this surely is a matter of primary importance and demands primacy in the church in all ages. This is the situation with respect to Galatians 3:26-29.

This passage is found in a letter where Paul constantly stresses the gospel and deals with the fundamental issue of how Jew and Greek come into a right relationship with God, and the implications for life resulting from a right relationship. Over against those who were troubling the Galatians with notions that faith in Christ is not sufficient for salvation, but that obedience to the law and the rite of circumcision are essential elements in becoming children of God, Paul emphasises the given nature of salvation through the redemptive work of Christ. There is therefore freedom from the law.[19] With the coming of Christ and the gift of faith in him, law has served its purpose for the Jew. Just as the Greek custodian/ disciplinarian (*paidagogos*) served a useful purpose till the child grew up and then became free from the slave's discipline and restraints, so now that faith has come, we (i.e. Paul and his Jewish readers) have freedom from the law. But Christ's work was not only for the benefit of Jews; the Gentiles (Greeks) in the Galatian congregations have also become the recipients of God's grace. Accordingly, he continues (3:26-29): 'For in Christ Jesus you are all the children of God...'

We are here confronted with the most fundamental doctrines of the Christian faith – baptism, faith, adoption into God's family, freedom from the law, unity in Christ. There can be no disputing that this passage is a most explicit statement concerning the enormous blessings which believers enjoy with God through being baptised into Christ. That is, Jew and Greek, slave and free, male and female, alike share in a deep unity in fellowship with all who have put on Christ.

The clear and succinct statement of the gospel in the Galatians passage is further emphasised by the fact that it is one of three Pauline statements encompassing the same gospel truths. Meeks and others have claimed, not without justification, that in Galatians 3:28, 1 Corinthians 12:13, and Colossians 3:10-11 there is to be found portion of a very ancient baptismal reunification liturgy.[20] The major motifs in the three passages are strikingly similar – baptism into Christ (or one body), putting on Christ (or the new man), the listing of two or more pairs of opposites and the declaration that all are one in Christ. Here then we have a most profound truth that Paul loved to repeat, a highly prized statement that he loved to quote, which had applications in different contexts in his letters.

The fact that it was located in a variety of contexts gives added value to it. This is not a hurriedly dashed off piece of apostolic teaching intended to meet the exigencies of some stressful situation (and thus with limited application as far as other contexts are concerned), but a statement of gospel principle, universally valid with applications to all manner of different contexts, a message to people divided, namely that this is your status – the children of God, you who are one in Christ Jesus through baptism. Consequently, instead of there being fragmentation and division resulting from different racial, religious, social and gender orientations, you people in Galatia are one in Christ!

Baptism and the gift of faith, oneness in Christ are the 'givens', caught up in the here and now situation where people stand apart on account of their race, religion, social status and gender. In Paul's time, as in ours, people were separated and divided from others in these areas. All these differences contain strong overtones of value judgments: one's race, or religion, or position in life, or sexuality are seen by many people to afford one status with God, or are regarded as placing one in a superior or inferior relationship with others.[21]

It was a theoretical commonplace that the Hellenistic man was grateful that he was born a human being and not a beast, a Greek and not a barbarian, a man and not a woman.[22] This 'insight' has sometimes been attributed to Plato who also claimed that women, no matter their age, could not think metaphysically. A rabbinic blessing that male Jews were expected to recite three times a day stated: 'Blessed (be he) that he did not create me a Gentile, that he did not create me a boor (a slave in the Babylonian Talmud), blessed be he that he did not create me a woman'. William Loader has highlighted that in ancient times women were often considered inferior to men:

> Women are not the same as men. Men are more experienced, more capable of controlling their emotions, more suited therefore to leadership in the public arena, and women are better taking on roles in the household.
> This appears to have been the assumption of most men in the Greco-Roman and Jewish world of the first century. It was a natural conclusion to draw, since most people married, and most men married women significantly younger than themselves, i.e. the man around 30 and the woman in her teens, sometimes half his age. Added to this the vulnerabilities related to frequent pregnancies and observations of physical strength, the male logic drew the following conclusions: women are inferior to us – flawed male reasoning which has survived well into our own day.[23]

For persons living under the old aeon where law is in control, one's status, both in the eyes of God and in the eyes of people in the community, is determined by considerations of race, religion, position in life and gender. The status of being a child of God through baptism into Christ frees the believer from trying unsuccessfully to present religion, race, status or anything else as a basis for why God should regard that person favourably, and it also frees the individual from trying to establish a superior self-image through favourable comparisons with others based on race, religion, sexual orientation and the like.

Overturning a World View

Scroggs spoke of the Christ event as the eschatological judgment of God on civilisation and its values.[24] This act, he said, also opens up the possibility of life, because the cross is God's acquittal of the man desperately caught up in, and therefore desperately proud of the web of the performance principle. When the performance principle is eliminated, so too is the significance of any roles or positions in society. As one stands before the giving God, all the old status symbols are meaningless, whether wealth, wisdom, religious activity, public approval, masculinity. Every person stands naked and guilty before God, but through baptism in Christ – equally acknowledged, established and free.

In Christ, Caird wrote, God has judged the world and found it wanting. In Christ, the new world order has been inaugurated, which was not simply a religious idea, but a new community, a new commonwealth, a new humanity.[25] In describing how all – Jew and Greek, slave and free, male and female – are one in Christ through baptism, there is the strong suggestion in Paul's writings of the church as the body of Christ – that marvellous concept developed more fully in his letters to the Corinthians and the Colossians. The oneness given in Christ, and which is of the essence of being his body, is demonstrated in caring, accepting, enabling and honouring of other members of the body. There are thus far-reaching consequences, both for the individual and for the community of believers, of being one in Christ, for an altogether new order of being has begun. God has brought into being this new creation. The devastating divisions resulting from the fall have no place in the new age for the body of Christ. Paul illustrates with three pairs of opposites that unity and equal honour can now be experienced and expressed by persons who, prior to their baptism in Christ, were painfully aware of division, alienation and fragmentation.

Neither Jew nor Greek

Since you are all one in Christ, Paul argues, there is therefore now 'neither Jew nor Greek'. Jews had the law and a long history of God's special involvement in their destiny. The Greeks had no such experience. Jews took great care not to become ceremoniously unclean through personal contact with Greeks whom they regarded as their religious inferiors, since the Greeks lacked the law and God's covenant relationship. But now that faith has come to both Jews and Greeks through their baptism in Christ, both now enjoy equal status with God through grace alone; there is now no place for one race to despise the other, or even to avoid social contact with the other.

Such a change from centuries of religious/social tradition of division did not come easily. Here was an area of real tension in early Christianity. For Paul, there were clearly very important religious and social implications for the Christian community since there was no longer 'neither Jew nor Greek'. These are clearly spelled out in his letter to the Galatians. Paul refused to allow Titus, a Greek, to submit to the rite of circumcision (Galatians 2:1-5). When Paul at Lystra circumcised Timothy (Acts 16:1-3), the situation was quite different. There was no pressure from Judaizers for the circumcision. Paul, with Timothy's concurrence, believed that since Timothy was the son of a Jewish mother, his ministry would be more effective among Jews if they prevented the matter of circumcision becoming an issue. Paul's main concern was that the gospel should be proclaimed without unnecessary hindrances. Cultural practices, Jewish laws and human traditions he did not regard as sacred idols; he discarded them when their observance would have obscured the truth of the gospel (Galatians 2:5) and he observed them when this enhanced the gospel proclamation (1 Corinthians 9:9-12). He refused to yield to the cultural and religious pressures exerted by over-zealous Jewish Christians 'that the truth of the gospel might be preserved' (Galatians 2:5). Paul's refusal was as revolutionary a break with religious and social practice as Peter's willingness to enter the home of Cornelius and to eat food in the home of Gentiles (Acts 10).

But an even more dramatic illustration of the profound social implications of 'neither Jew nor Greek' can be seen from Paul's public reprimand of Peter at Antioch. During a visit to that city, Cephas had at first associated freely and publicly with Gentile Christians, but then when Jewish Christians arrived at Antioch who were closely aligned with James, Peter rejected the unity he had earlier expressed towards Gentile Christians and practised fellowship now only with

Jewish Christians. What was at stake was something more fundamental than the hypocrisy of an important leader of the church. Paul considered it an open repudiation of the gospel (Galatians 2:11ff). Peter's conduct at Antioch was a blatant denial that both Jew and Gentile believers are one in Christ; it was as though the law was still in force for Jews, and Greeks were outside the covenant relationship. The equality of Jew and Greek before God had to be lived out and expressed in the social setting of interpersonal relationships. For Peter to persist in avoiding contact with Gentile Christians, because of pressure from Jewish conservatives, would have made him guilty of repudiating the truth about God's saving activity in Christ. 'To revert to kosher observance in social relationships is to give up the freedom for which Christ died; it is to deny the new reality Christ brings to a newly unified humankind (Galatians 2:11 to 5:1). In the case of Jew and Greek, then, the new humanity has constituted a new present social reality for Paul'.[26]

Caird saw the significance of Peter's action and Paul's public repudiation of his apostolic partner as issues with fundamental importance for the church:

> If 'neither Jew nor Greek' meant nothing more than equal access to the throne of grace, Paul's long-running battle with Judaizers, his determined struggles to maintain unity between Jewish and Gentile Christianity, the crusade which prompted his collection for the Jerusalem church and which cost him his liberty and in the end his life – all this need never have happened. On the contrary, the certain fact is that Paul conceived the new unity of Jew and Gentile in Christ in terms of a new commonwealth of Israel. The idea

that the new life in Christ was simply religious and must not be allowed to interfere with existing social patterns was precisely the line adopted by Peter and Barnabas on the famous occasion when Paul withstood Peter to his face (Galatians 2:11ff).[27]

Whereas there may be some room for debate whether Paul had thought through all the social and religious implications for the here and now situation of the two other sets of opposites (slave and free, male and female), there is no doubt that 'neither Jew nor Greek' affected him personally and directly in the very life and structure of the church. So seriously did he view the implications that this gospel truth had for the life of the Christian community, that he was prepared to run the risk of adding to the tension of an inflamed situation (to say nothing of the humiliation caused to the leading church apostle of the day) by publicly reprimanding Peter for his denial of the truth by his two-faced behaviour.

Neither Slave nor Free

As indicated, it is not certain whether Paul appreciated the radical implications of 'neither slave nor free'. Stendahl said that the translation of 1 Corinthians 7:21 remains 'an insoluble problem'.[28] However, if the context of the Corinthian text is any guide, it may be argued that Paul is encouraging slaves to remain in their servitude, even if the chance of liberty should come their way. An important principle Paul reiterates in the context is that 'each should continue as he was when God's call came to him' (7:17, 20, 24). It is also probable that the motivation for the instruction given concerning marriage and life generally in the world (25-31) is at the back of Paul's mind when he instructs slaves. 'Our time is growing short', he says, and again 'the world as we know it is passing away' (7:29, 31). Paul's expectation of an imminent Parousia shaped his thinking about life in this present world. If one expected eschatological deliverance at any moment, it is unlikely that one would be giving slaves instruction to emancipate themselves. They would soon experience a far more wonderful freedom!

In Colossians 3:22 to 4:1 and Ephesians 6:5-9, the writer (presumably Paul) emphasised the new dimension in the master-slave relationship: both stand in a shared relationship over against Christ. The old relationship must cease in that the slave thinks of himself as one who exists simply to please his master (Ephesians 6:6); rather, because of the cross, he must see himself as the servant of Christ; likewise, the master must see himself as under a master in heaven.[29] Paul's letter to Philemon contains no explicit statement that slavery is incompatible with the gospel and that Philemon must release his runaway slave, Onesimus. There is, however, a new dimension to their relationship since they are now brothers in the Lord. Perhaps Paul is hinting that Philemon ought to release Onesimus without explicitly asking him to do so.

It would have been totally unrealistic for Paul to advocate the freeing of slaves; even if he had such a conviction (which is rather unlikely), it would have been an exercise in futility for a handful of scattered Christian communities, lacking power and influence, to attempt to change the deeply entrenched social and political reality of slavery. Slaves represented a high proportion in the many Roman provinces and the whole economic fabric of Roman life was dependent on their existence. Paul did not set out to rid his world of slavery (just as he did not seek to rid Jew and Greek of their racial identity, or males and females of their gender identity), but in the statement 'neither slave nor free' a truth was stated which Christians later understood as a call to rid society of an evil practice.[30] Paul saw the here and now implications of 'neither slave nor free' in terms of the respect and concern with which both classes should regard and treat one another because of their shared relationship in Christ.

Later generations of Christians have rightly seen the implications of this statement in terms of the elimination of the whole institution of slavery. 'Neither slave nor free' has come to mean that not only in the sight of God, but also in the Americas, Australia and Siberia there is no place for attitudes and practices that are a denial of human equality. While the abolition of slavery became a reality only after some nineteen centuries of gospel proclamation, and whilst the absence of explicit rejection of slavery by Paul was used for centuries by pro-slavery advocates as scriptural justification for its continuance, one would surely not find the attitude today even among the most emphatic supporters of the *coram deo* interpretation of Galatians 3:28, that the occurrence of slavery is no longer a concern for the Christian church.

Admittedly, it has taken the Holy Spirit a long time to enlighten Christians (and to overcome the opposition of slave owners and slave traders) to rid them of the notion that slavery is some sort of permanent order established by the Creator. Thank God, one would not find in our time any child of God so insensitive to the social and moral implications of 'neither slave nor free' who would claim 'let the secular world and the United Nations fight slavery, but let the church follow its conscience and limit Galatians 3:28 to the realm of pure concern for man's individual salvation, without any meddlesome involvement in political and social matters'.[31] 'Neither slave nor free' has become a blueprint for social action, and there is no doubt in my mind that such an understanding of the passage is a legitimate application of the gospel principle in vastly different and political environments.

Neither Male nor Female

The third dyad, 'neither male nor female' is addressing the most primary division in humankind. Instead of writing 'There is neither man nor woman' as one would expect following the other dyads, Paul uses the LXX (Greek version) of Genesis 1:27 and interrupts the sequence of 'neither ...nor ...' with what seems like a quotation from Genesis 1 creation narrative 'There is 'no male and female'(*arsen kai thely*).[32] This is the only occasion where Paul refers to the creation narrative, which emphasises that humankind as 'male and female' was created in the image of God. Among rabbinic writers, Genesis 2 was most commonly used, undoubtedly because it is possible to read into the Genesis 2 account support for their notion of woman's subjection to man.[33] Genesis 1, however, clearly and most emphatically repudiates such a suggestion, stressing the equality of male and female in the image of God.

The most fundamental difference between people, their gender, which is an essential part of God's creation, is the area in which there are and always have been sharpest divisions, disunity, injustices and inequality. In and through the second Adam, these divisions and injustices, which have their origin in a person's gender, are removed. For in Christ there is not male and female, but persons of different sexuality one in Christ. The whole of humanity is divided into male and female – the primary division – but even it must give way to unity for those who have put on Christ in baptism.[34] It is hardly necessary to point out that Paul is not advocating the elimination of human gender, just as he is not advocating that Jews should cease being Jews and Greeks cease being Greeks and become something else instead. Whilst retaining their maleness or their femaleness, it is possible for them to be one in Christ.[35]

That Paul is speaking about something more than the relationship male and female have with God ought to be obvious. If that were all it was supposed to mean, then it would have been a most apparent truism. Though the Jewish faith was patriarchal and women were restricted in the exercise of their faith, there is no doubt that Jewish women had the same access to God, and were acceptable or unacceptable to God on the same basis, or for the same reasons as Jewish males.[36] Miriam, Hannah, Mary (the mother of our Lord), Mary of Magdala clearly illustrate that they shared equally with men in God's grace and mercy. If then 'neither male nor female' has to do with *coram deo* only, then it is saying the most obvious fact, which no one of Jewish faith ever questioned. Nor is there any suggestion that among the Galatians, or in any other congregation for that matter, there was some dispute in this regard.

What then would have been the purpose of such a pair of opposites if it was intended to stress that which everyone took for granted? There never was any doubt that in God's sight men and women shared equally in the image of God, shared equally in the fall into sin and shared equally in the covenant of grace God held out to them in Christ. Though some rabbis tended to question the extent to which women were in God's image, and also tended to blame woman for humankind's sin, Paul's third pair 'neither male nor female' would have been a monumental anti-climax after the previous pairs of opposites, if it was intended to convey nothing more than that men and women through baptism are one in Christ.

Cultural and Religious Background

A consideration of the cultural and religious background to Paul's writings is crucial to this discussion. When Paul wrote that both male and female are one, united and equal in their relationship with God through baptism, he was writing from a background and into a cultural and religious setting that flatly rejected any notion of a woman having equal honour and equal recognition with man.[37] In the here and now of social and religious life in the community, in both Jewish and Gentile contexts, women were regarded and treated as subordinate to men, and therefore also inferior. At the beginning of the Common Era, women were exempt from the study of the law. Rabbi Eliezer maintained that to teach one's daughter the Torah was to teach her lechery, and that the Torah ought to be burned rather than given to women.

In the temple of Herod, women were permitted to enter only the women's court. This was five steps above that of the heathen, and fifteen steps below the court for men, which women were not permitted to enter. Women were permitted to enter their court only by certain gates – but even this was not permitted if they were within seven days of the end of their menstruation, or forty days since the birth of a son, or eighty days since the birth of a daughter. In the synagogues used in Palestine, and throughout the diaspora, women were restricted either to a screened balcony above the worshipping men, or were confined to a separate adjoining room.

Along with children under the age of thirteen and slaves, women could not constitute the necessary quorum of ten to form a congregation to worship communally. Even if nine men were available and fifty women, this did not constitute the necessary quorum. Women were not permitted to read the Torah at the synagogue worship. Not surprisingly then, Jewish men, seemingly almost universally (for the prayer is found in widely scattered rabbinic collections), praised God that God had not created them Gentiles, ignoramuses and women because women were not obliged to fulfil the commandments. In his description of women, Philo used such expressions as weak, easily deceived, the cause of sin, lifeless, diseased, enslaved, unmanly, nerveless, mean, slavish and sluggish. He saw the husband's relationship to his wife like that of a father to his children and the owner to his slaves. The proper relation of wife to husband was expressed, Philo taught, by the Greek word *douleuein* 'to serve as a slave'.[38]

Among the Greeks, there were widely different attitudes and practices over against women in social and religious life. The Epicureans sought to create a 'communal existence in which the normal social roles of the sexes were abolished and male and female were equal', but there were exceptions. Women were permitted to take part in the Greek athletic contests of the first century before Christ and were allowed to take part in the initiation ceremonies at Eleusis. Plato, though he advocated education for girls as well as for boys, regarded women as inferior by nature to men.[39]

A Radical Message

Paul's readers could not help but be struck by the radical and revolutionary nature of what he was declaring, when he wrote that there is not male and female but one in Christ. There was no way his readers could have avoided the social and religious implications of his statement, since it was addressed to a social environment that took for granted that between men and women there was not equality and unity, but fundamental differences in roles, status and function. But Paul wrote that sexuality – maleness or femaleness – is not the basis by which a person can claim a position of superiority or advantage to which another is not entitled – neither in his relationship with God, nor with respect to another human being.

To rephrase: In Christ it is not sexuality that is abolished, but the antagonism and the injustices that have resulted from half the world's population being male and the other half female. If one's gender does not count in respect to God and if persons of different gender are truly one in Christ, the way is cleared for male and female to begin to express and experience in Christ's body, the fellowship and unity God intended when God created male and female in the image of God. Christ's redemptive work was directed towards rescuing humankind from the curse resulting from the fall into sin.[40] Part of that curse for woman was to be denied the equality with man in which she was created. This is now restored through her partnership in the gospel through baptism. God's new age has thus broken in upon the world through Christ. Though Paul well knew that the old aeon was still a reality to be endured with hope, the new age was for him also a present reality, not only some future event.[41] For those who have been baptised into Christ it was as though the bell-lap of world history had been sounded, and one of the characteristics of this new age is that there is reunification through baptism in Christ for such opposites as Jew and Greek, slave and free, male and female.[42]

Paul Under Scrutiny

It was shown earlier that, where Paul through personal experience saw a threat to the gospel as in the Greek/Gentile Jewish tensions at Antioch, he very emphatically claims and acts on the new liberty inherent in his declaration that in Christ there is neither Greek nor Jew, slave nor free, male nor female. In the life and structure of the Pauline congregations, 'neither Jew nor Greek' found dynamic expression. What of 'neither male nor female'? The attitude and teaching of Paul in respect to women continues to be an area of considerable debate among New Testament scholars, and Scroggs was probably right when he claimed that 'the trouble with Paul is that he has too many friends and too many enemies' just in this area.[43]

There are three major problems facing the biblical scholar as they seek to determine what were the social implications for Paul of his 'neither male nor female' statement.

The first is to determine which are the genuine Pauline passages in the New Testament that deal with this subject. This important matter will be considered in more detail in connection with the study of 1 Timothy 2:8-15 in Chapter 4. In passing, it should be stated that even if the Pauline authorship of this passage could be disproved, the implications for the life and practice of the church today in respect to 1 Timothy would still have to be seriously considered. For it is ultimately not a question of what Paul wrote, but what is the teaching of the New Testament canon. However, if one is concerned primarily with the teaching and practice of Paul on the subject of women's place in church and society, then the question of the genuineness of this passage has to be a major consideration.

The second problem is that Paul did not seek to provide a detailed discussion on the role of women in the ministry of women in the early church, but only limited and occasional information. We have fragments of information about the early church which have surfaced because Paul was dealing with particular problems in local congregations (as when Paul wrote to the people at Corinth), or information that has come down to us as a result of greetings the apostle extended to men and women in various Christian communities.[44] To try to construct a theology for our time from such meagre information demands a great amount of caution.

The third problem is closely related to androcentric perspectives at work and has been referred to earlier. It is the real difficulty of trying to read the New Testament without the patriarchal, androcentric perspectives that can seriously restrict one's understanding of the writings in question. Elizabeth Schüssler-Fiorenza gave some interesting examples of how androcentric perspectives and presuppositions have interfered with a complete picture emerging from the New Testament documents.[45] Bernadette Brooten has shown how commentators have changed the sexual identity of one of the persons Paul describes as 'outstanding among the apostles' (Romans 16:7).[46] The person whose gender is disputed is Junia – but Junias for those who insist that this person has to be a male to be described as 'outstanding among the apostles.'

The evidence suggests otherwise. Origin of Alexandria, the earliest commentator on Romans 16:7, considered the name to be that of a female (Junia or Julia). John Chrysostom, Jerome, Theophylact, Abelard all agreed. It was only in the 13th century when it was first suggested by Aediqius that the two persons in the passage were men (*viri*). His reason was that the reading of Juliam was to be preferred to Juniam, since 'apostles' had to be male, and he mistakenly thought that Julia was a male name. Luther relying on Faber Stapulensis, took the accusative Jounian to be Julias – a masculine name – a hypothesis adopted widely since his time. Not all commentators, however, agree. Lagrange argued on textual grounds for the feminine Junia. Brooten claimed that there is not a single shred of evidence that the name Junias ever existed.

It seems then that commentators' presuppositions concerning the gender of apostles have prevented the reality of Paul's statement from being heard in our time. Since it was considered inconceivable that a woman could be described as an outstanding apostle, the person was given a different gender and name![47] Schüssler-Fiorenza has claimed:

> New Testament writers did not incorporate all available information into their works, but have selected the materials according to their own theological purposes... Paul's letters refer to women as co-missionaries, whereas Acts only mentions the contributions that wealthy women gave as patronesses, but does not picture them as missionaries... While all four gospels know of Mary Magdalene as the first witness to the resurrection, Paul does not list any women among the resurrection witnesses. Or: the fourth gospel claims that a woman had an important role in the beginning of the Samaritan mission (John

4:4-42), whereas Acts mentions Philip as the first missionary in Samaria (Acts 8:4-13). Since the NT authors write from an androcentric point of view and select their information accordingly, we can conjecture that they transmit a small fraction of the information ... on women available to them. Therefore, the sparse NT references to women do not at all reflect adequately women's actual role and contribution to the history of early Christianity. They allow us, however, a glimpse of the possibly rich traditions which we have lost.[48]

Females in Ministry in New Testament Times

Despite the incomplete nature of the New Testament evidence, there is sufficient data supplied to show us that in the ministry and life of the early church there was a very real awareness of the far-reaching implications of Paul's insight that in Christ there is 'neither male nor female'. It is of considerable importance that it is Paul – in some quarters considered the most notorious of male chauvinists – who demonstrated even in the culturally restricted climate of his time, that the unity and equality of male and female through Christ can find expression in the work and witness of the Christian assembly.

It has been the normal practice to pass over in very summary manner the reference to women in the congregations of the early church, as though their role was minor. If, however, we take into account the very strong cultural prejudices against women (especially against women's involvement in public affairs outside the home), the evidence supplied by Paul (and others) strongly suggests that women were involved in a quite extensive and prominent way in various forms of ministry in the early church.[49] The characterisation of these women and their work in no way suggests that they were dependent on Paul or subordinate to him. Paul uses titles and descriptions of various women that stress the missionary nature of the labours.

He calls Prisca a 'co-worker' (Romans 16:3), Apphia 'our sister' (Philemon 2), Phoebe 'our sister, a *diakonos* of the church, a *prostatis* of many and of myself' (Romans 16:1-2), and Junia or Julia as a 'leader among the apostles' (Romans 16:7). Paul quite indiscriminately uses the same words (*synergein, synergos, kopian*) not only to characterise his missionary labours, but also in reference to the work which women were carrying out in the church: Romans 16:6, 12 Mary, Tryphana, Tryphosa and Persis; 1 Corinthians 15:10; 1 Thessalonians 5:12 – 'those who work among you and are over you in the Lord'; 1 Corinthians 16:16 – 'every fellow worker and labourer'; Romans 16:3 – Prisca and Aquila 'fellow workers'. *Synergoi* is the noun used of men who played an important part in the early church – Timothy (Romans 16:21), Apollos and Paul (1 Corinthians 3:9, Titus (2 Corinthians 8:23).In his letter to the Philippians Paul affirms that Euodia and Syntyche have contended side by side with him, as team members in a contest, along with Clement and the other missionaries. These women whose influence in the congregation was obviously very considerable, since Paul feared their continued dissension would cause serious harm, are given the same esteem and respect as male co-workers at Philippi (4:2-3).

Phoebe is mentioned at the head of a list of 27 persons in Romans 16, and what he says of her and what he expects of his readers in respect to this woman in no way suggests any subordination on her part, rather subordination to her

(Romans 16:1-2). She is to be received worthily and is to be helped in whatever way she requires. Paul uses three titles for this woman: 'sister' – if 'brother' can be used for missionary co-workers (Philippians 4:21ff), then 'sister' would be the appropriate title for a female co-worker; whenever Paul uses this word in reference to himself or another male leader it is translated as 'minister', 'missionary', 'servant', or 'deacon', but when it comes to Phoebe the word is rendered 'deaconess', or as 'a fellow Christian who holds office in the congregation'. Using the title 'deaconess' immediately suggests an office which developed centuries later in the church. Paul did not describe her as *diakonissa* but as *diakonos*. That Phoebe held a position of prominence and authority, like that of any other *diakonos* in the church, is beyond question when the third title is considered – *prostatis*.[50] It is commonly translated in such a weak way that it is deprived of its real meaning – 'helper' in the RSV, and 'good friend' in the Good News Bible.

Prostatis is not found elsewhere in the New Testament. It is the feminine form of *prostates* and is derived from the verb *proistemi*. The masculine word was used to mean, in other writings of the time, a first-rank person, a leader, a chief, ruler, president or presiding officer, guardian champion, a patron who provided protection. In the LXX (Septuagint), the masculine form is used of the stewards of David's property (1 Chronicles 27:31), of officers over the king's work (1 Chronicles 29:6), of the chief officer who exercised authority over the people (2 Chronicles 8:10), of Phineas, the leader of the sanctuary (Sirach 45:24), and of Simon, the governor of the temple (2 Maccabees 3:4). Its verb form is used in 1 Thessalonians 5:12 in respect to persons in authority in the congregation, and in 1 Timothy 3:4f and 5:17 it designates the function of the bishop, deacon or elder. In view of the above evidence, to describe Phoebe as 'helper' is totally inadequate, for the word used invariably describes a person with authority and major responsibility. Phoebe is clearly presented as a person in a position of actual leadership in the church – and her authority was widely respected, certainly also by Paul himself.[51]

Another female person deserving of special mention is Prisca. Paul describes her (along with her husband Aquilla) as *synergoi*, a term which Paul uses interchangeably with *diakonoi* as in 1 Corinthians 3:5,9 and 1 Thessalonians 3:2 (variant reading). Whenever Paul sends greetings to Prisca and Aquilla, he mentions Prisca first (Romans 16:3f; 2 Timothy 4:19). Luke also mentions Prisca ahead of her husband in Acts 18:2ff and 18:26 – both writers attesting to the leadership role fulfilled by this woman, who among other forms of ministry instructed Apollos in the full truth of the gospel. All the infant churches (along with Paul himself) had good reason to give thanks to God for missionary leaders Prisca and Aquilla. Their house churches in Corinth, Ephesus and Rome were the centre for church life and worship.

It is thus obvious from the above detailed description that in the Pauline congregations, women exercised important functions of ministry.[52] As will be shown later, even in Corinth where wives are instructed not to speak, women were prominent in public worship through prophecy and prayer (1 Corinthians 11:5). Thus, while male leaders are much more prominent in the record presented in the New Testament, there is more than sufficient evidence to demonstrate that 'neither male nor female' found early expression in the Pauline churches, in spite of the historic religious and cultural obstacles and barriers that needed to be overcome. Thus, in the church of the first century, action was being taken by women and men to demonstrate that the Judaeo-religious limitations on women were invalid and were on the way out. In the life of Paul's congregations, women worked and served, prayed and taught, evangelised and prophesised side by side with men, both truly one and equal before God through their baptism into Christ.

William Loader, in drawing attention to the role played by women in the church's early years, e.g. Romans 16: Prisca, Mary, Junia ('prominent among the apostles' 16:7), Tryphaena and Tryphosa (16:3-12), commented ('Social Justice and Gender'):

> It is not altogether surprising in a movement which had its beginnings not among the male elite but among the poor, that the disempowered would assume roles not normally allowed them in the public arena. Women were part of Jesus' itinerant group (Mark 15:40-41; 3:31-35; 10:30; Luke 8:2-3), not just key players in hosting the itinerants in their homes (Mark 1:29-31; Luke 10:38-42; John 12:1-8). Is Magdala not a place but a nickname 'the tower' given by Jesus to Mary, as Jesus gave Simon the nickname Cephas/Petros, 'the rock', as Joan Taylor has suggested?' Given the movement's origins, it is understandable that women played a more significant role in the movement in the early decades than normally allotted to them in society. As Gentiles flooded in, pressure mounted to abandon the biblical requirement of circumcision set out in Genesis 17. They did. We find two independent accounts of the meeting in Jerusalem where they did just that (Galatians 2:1-10; Acts 15:1-21), though not without

controversy (cf. Galatians 5:2-12). Such pressure did not, however, succeed in subverting the norms about women. The pressure to return to normal was too great.[53]

It is worth noting here a recent LCA assessment of women in ministry in Paul's day. In a background paper 'A theological basis for the ordination of women and men: Background to the draft doctrinal statement' prepared by the Commission on Theology and Inter-Church Relations (CTICR) prior to the synod of the Lutheran Church in Australia in 2018, the summary observation was made, after describing in detail how women were engaged in ministry in the New Testament churches:

> So, although there were a variety of models for leadership and a variety of ways of ordering ministry in the early church, these examples show that in some locations, women were included in major leadership and ministry roles. Indeed, the New Testament provides substantial evidence that women were numbered along with the apostles (Junia), prophets (the women in Corinth, Philip's daughters), evangelists (Euodia and Syntyche), church planters (Mary, Traephena and Tryphosa), deacons/ministers (Phoebe) and teachers (Priscilla). These factors play an important role in helping us to understand why women may become pastors today. In affirming the ordination of women, the LCA would be following the witness and precedent of the New Testament with regard to women in ministry.[54]

Summary Conclusion

I began a consideration of Paul's statement in Galatians 3:26-29 by raising the question: Is the writer of that letter intent on doing nothing more than describing how it is for Jew and Greek, slave and free, male and female in their relationship with God, or is he wanting his readers to also consider implications in the here and now of how Jew and Greek, slave and free, male and female might live out and express their unity in Christ and with one another in church and society? In the ministry of Paul himself and in his writings he demonstrated that there are important consequences for the lives for all those who 'are the children of God through faith...'. Having been 'baptised into Christ' and 'having clothed themselves with Christ,' unity can now take the place of disunity for people who were previously divided on account of their religious background, their social status and their gender. This new-found unity he expressed in bringing Jew and Gentile together, in spite of the centuries of cultural and religious division; for slaves and their masters he highlighted the new dimension in their relationship; the unity and equality of male and female he demonstrated by encouraging and honouring women to share fully in leadership roles in the infant church.[55]

In Paul's dramatic gospel declaration that, as a consequence of sharing in a unique unity through being baptised in Christ, the church also in our time has compelling motivation to apply the 'neither male nor female' declaration to ensure that women do not continue to be discriminated against in the life and ministry of today's church.

Chapter 3
The Silence Expected of Wives in the Worship at Corinth

ONE OF THE TWO PASSAGES USED REPEATEDLY by the LCA for the past 70 years in its defence of refusing to permit women from becoming ministers of the Word and sacraments is 1 Corinthians 14:34-35:

> As in all the churches of the saints, wives should be silent in the churches. For they are not permitted to speak, but should be subordinate, as the law also says. If there is anything they desire to know, let them ask their husbands at home. For it is shameful for a woman to speak in church. Or did the word of God originate with you? Or are you the only ones it has reached?[56]

It was a dramatic reversal when in 2018, the Commission on Theology and Church Relations (CTICR) of the LCA issued a statement 'The Theological Basis for the Ordination of Women and Men: Draft Doctrinal Statement' in which they declared: 'Since 1 Timothy 2:11-14 and 1 Corinthians 14:33b-37 do not specifically address the issue of ordination, they cannot be used to support the exclusion of women from the pastoral office'.[57]

Since the Synod in convention a few months later failed to provide the necessary two-thirds majority needed to endorse the recommendation to approve the ordination of women and men, it is assumed that within the LCA a significant number of pastors and lay persons continue to maintain that these passages prevent women from becoming ordained ministers in the LCA. In the following pages, I provide my analysis from 40 years ago to demonstrate that the 2018 judgment of the CTICR was soundly based and deserving of support.

The Corinthian Setting

These verses come near the end of a lengthy section dealing with the problems in the worship life of the charismatic congregation at Corinth (11:2 to 14:40). The rich outpouring of the gifts of the Spirit and the resultant difficulties in handling these gifts provided the setting for specific instructions from Paul. He was forced to address a situation that would be totally foreign to us who are accustomed to a highly structured liturgical worship experience. The very worship life of the congregation was seriously at risk because of the disorder, confusion (and probably noise!). Repeatedly, he stresses in chapter 14 that worshippers should be edified through their participation in worship and that good order should prevail.[58] 'Let all things be done for edification' (14:26) and 'let all things be done decently and in order' (14:40) provide a powerful framework for the instruction he gives. What was going on in that unruly congregation was obviously a blatant repudiation of the apostle's intention that the church should be built up in faith, hope and love (1 Corinthians 13:13; 14:3-5, 12, 17).

Paul's directions to wives are a part of a series of instructions given to persons involved in that congregation's worship. Rules are given for those 'speaking in tongues' (14:27ff), for prophets (14:29-32) and then for wives (14:34-35), so that some much-needed order might be established instead of the free-wheeling, unstructured worship experience. The two key verbs used in reference to wives are used frequently throughout the chapter. These are the words 'to be silent' (*sigan*) as in verses 28, 30 and 34, and 'to speak' (*lalein*) as in verses 2-7, 11, 13, 18, 19, 21, 23, 27-29, 34, 35, 39. With the exception of verses 3, 11, 28, 29, 34, 35, *lalein* occurs in this chapter with 'in tongues', either stated clearly or clearly implied. The nature of the speaking in verses 34-35 is explained in 35a as having to do with asking their husbands questions.

Dealing with the Disorder

It would seem that considerable discussion followed a prophetic utterance or an ecstatic speech and this was disturbing, confusing and unedifying, especially if several spoke at once. One of the measures to which Paul resorted to bring some order out of the disorder was to insist that wives should remain silent in the chaos and ask their husbands at home if they needed information or instruction on what was being said. The sort of speaking that they were engaged in was in contrast to, even a repudiation of, their being subordinate to their husbands.

Subordination would be demonstrated by wives not talking, not raising questions, but by their silence. Subordination to their husbands was a requirement of the law, Paul states. What law it was, he does not state – certainly there was no such law or requirement demanding subordination of wives in the Old Testament. It is, therefore, obvious that Paul's long participation in synagogue worship provided the background for him to state that this was required by the law. Certainly, in the synagogue the rule was strongly maintained that wives must be silent as a sign that they were subordinate to their husbands.[59] This regulation to reduce the chaos in worship by demanding that wives be silent (as was generally the practice in synagogue worship) did not conflict with an earlier decree in chapter 11 that wives who were engaged in prophecy and prayer in worship did not do injury to the 'proper' relationship with their husbands, if they wore the appropriate head-dress – that is the head-dress expected of prophetesses. But those wives who were not engaged in prophecy and prayer and who did not wear the appropriate head-dress, should remember their station in life, and be subordinate to their husbands by not engaging in 'garrulous questioning concerning the interpretation of prophecy'.[60] Loader observed in *The New Testament on Sexuality* (p. 388):

> Recognising the Jewish background to Paul's values in this matter, as in the matter of hair covering, helps to resolve the contrast between what he writes in 11:5 and 14:33b-36. For the same Judaism of which he was a part could at the same time recognise that women may be inspired to take on leadership roles, including those of the prophet. What we see juxtaposed in 1 Corinthians is therefore much like what we see juxtaposed in Judaism, in which Paul is at home and whose values he espouses, except where perceived divine instruction has taught him otherwise. As in

Jewish communities, normally women would be expected to be silent, so this was to apply in the churches, which, at least in the beginning, understood themselves as Jewish communities anyway. As in Jewish life there were exceptions where women were inspired to leadership, so in the Christian communities there were inspired women exercising ministry, including that of prophecy. Paul did not conclude that all women were so inspired, but apparently had no difficulty in the fact that some were, provided that they dressed appropriately.

Not Parallel Statements

In linking 1 Corinthians 14:34-35 with 1 Timothy 2:11-15 to provide a Scriptural basis for the exclusion of women from the public ministry of the church, the LCA apparently saw the two statements as parallel, as though both were teaching the same thing. Whether the Timothy passage teaches the exclusion of women from the ministry will be considered and rejected in the following chapter. If we look closely at the words used in both passages, it becomes clear that they are addressing totally different issues. In Corinthians, wives are forbidden to 'speak' (*lalein*), whereas in Timothy they are forbidden to 'teach' (*didaskein*). But whenever *lalein* is used by Paul in the sense of teach, it has an object that specifies the sort of teaching that is taking place. Thus, in 1 Thessalonians 2:2 'to speak to you the gospel of God' (*lalesai pros hyman to evangelium*). Furthermore, not even the most garrulous talking by the Corinthian wives approached the reprehensible conduct implicit in the Timothy passage 'have authority over men' (*authentein andros*).[61]

Furthermore, another compelling reason for rejecting the notion that 1 Corinthians 14:34-35 and 1 Timothy 2:11-15 are parallel passages prohibiting women from being called into the public ministry of the church, is that they are addressed to totally different situations. In the former, the apostle is determined to bring some order into the chaotic worship life of the Corinthian congregation; in the Timothy passage, the writer is intent on imposing silence on women whose teaching was characterised by a word (*authentein*) which would make that sort of teaching out of order also for men – a teaching that was presumably false.[62] The situations are totally different in spite of the superficial similarity in certain phrases employed. Clearly then, they are not parallel statements addressing the same issue.

The Weight of the Cultural Context

To use 1 Corinthians 14:34-35 as the Scriptural basis for prohibiting women from entering the service of their Lord as pastors, the passage would have to be free from any suggestion that it is culturally shaped and determined. If some principle was being established which the church of all time was bound to adhere to, this would need to be stated, and the basis for the rule would need to be related to the ageless truth of the gospel of God's grace in Christ. But such criteria are clearly not found in the Corinthian text. The basis for the instruction given to the Corinthians is not gospel-related, but culturally determined.

Paul's rationale is that when wives were speaking in response to some prophecy or preaching, they were not behaving in accordance with women being subordinate to men, which the law demands (i.e. the practice in Jewish synagogues demands). They should ask their husbands at home. Their behaviour was shameful! That he should designate the behaviour of these wives as shameful gives a valuable insight into the apostle's thinking and motivation for the direction he gives. In a male-dominating society, it was shameful for wives to step out of line and not show their husbands the deference and subservience expected of them – the very thing these Corinthians' wives were doing by asking questions and discussing in public the interpretation of prophetic speech.

In Corinth in the first century, such behaviour was shameful. But in our day in most churches it would not be shameful for wives in a Bible study group, or public meeting, or similar setting, to disagree with their husbands about the interpretation of a biblical passage. Presumably some husbands might be threatened by a different understanding of the point at issue, but there would be many others who have encouraged a relationship of honesty, openness and trust with their wives, and who would feel disappointed if their wives did not feel free to express different views.

No Parallel to Women in Ministry Today

It should be apparent that Paul was not dealing with a situation that in any way parallels our structured worship services, when he told the wives not to speak but to ask their husbands at home. What those wives were doing was shameful, given the demands made on women in that culture. It was not shameful for wives to prophesy and pray and teach, provided the social norms in respect to their husbands were complied with. As was shown in chapter 2, in Pauline congregations women did figure prominently in a variety of roles, which are parallel to the public teaching of the Word and the administration of the sacraments in our churches. Paul's obvious approval of them and endorsement of their ministries is fully in accord with his basic theological insight that in Christ there is 'neither male nor female'. But when dealing with a very distressing and complicated situation where the worship life of the congregation was threatened by a variety of disorders, including the repudiation of the socially accepted structure that wives must be subordinate to their husbands, he insists that such wives must be silent. The reasons he advances for this desired outcome reflect the cultural, social and religious contexts of his world.

It is in no way surprising or even inappropriate for Paul to draw on his background as a Jew and refer to rabbinic teaching and synagogue practice, for his feelings of shame must have been determined by such a heritage. If Paul had argued that women talking in the service was incompatible with the gospel, or if he had contended that what these garrulous women were doing was an attempt to overthrow the truth, then there would have been an altogether different basis for his instructions, and their normative value for his time and for ours would have been immeasurably strengthened.

The normative value of this passage for our day may be likened to other instructions which the apostle gives in the same chapter, such as regulations for speaking in tongues, their interpretation, prophecy, the number of speakers and such like. We have elsewhere in the writings of the apostles, instructions for the church then, which we do not consider binding or applicable for Christians today. Examples of this are: instructions for slaves (Colossians 4:22; 1 Timothy 6:1-2; 1 Corinthians 7:21-22; Titus 2:9-11); the appropriate head-dress for men and women (1 Corinthians 11:2-16); the way women should dress when going to worship (1 Timothy 2:9); the enrolling of young widows (1 Timothy 5:11); being unequally yoked with unbelievers (2 Corinthians 6:14); the celibate life preferable (1 Corinthians 7:8-9); the unqualified obedience to be given to Caesar (Romans 13).

In maintaining that the cultural, social and religious environment evoked specific responses from New Testament writers, I am not minimising the importance of their responses to these situations, nor is there any suggestion that the Holy Spirit was somehow less involved in what they wrote. The task confronting the church in every age is to determine what is the authoritative Word of God for us in our culture, in our specific setting, time and place. It is surely obvious that to apply what Paul wrote about the behaviour of wives in the Corinthian congregation, who were not showing subordination to their husbands, to the situation in our day when equality of the sexes is an established norm, and use that instruction as a basis to prohibit women from becoming ordained ministers in the church, is a serious misuse of Scripture. It is clearly a case where a passage of Scripture addressed to wives who were not showing due deference to their husbands by speaking in church is plainly misapplied, if used as a reason for not permitting women to become ministers in our time. It was also a misapplication of this text in the past, when used to prohibit women from becoming elders, synodical delegates, lay preachers as well as pastors. It was being used to do something for which it was never intended.

Comments that Luther made in a sermon entitled 'How Christians should read Moses' are worth serious consideration in this context as well:

> One must handle and deal with the Scriptures soberly. The Word originally came into being in many different ways. One must not only observe if it is God's word, or if God has spoken it, but also to whom it was spoken. Does it concern you, or someone else? Here is a distinction like that between summer and winter. God said many things to David; he commanded this and that. But it does not apply to me, it has not been spoken to me. He could well have it speak to me, had he wanted to. You must observe the word that concerns you, that which is spoken to you and does not concern anyone else. There are two kinds of words in Scripture. The one that does not apply to me, nor does it concern me. The other does concern me and upon this one which concerns me, I may venture boldly and depend on it as upon a strong rock. If it does not concern me, I must stand still. The false prophets come and say, 'Dear people, this is the Word of God!' That is true, we cannot deny it, but we are not the people to whom it speaks.[63]

Chapter 4

The Teaching Forbidden to Wives
1 Timothy 2:8-15

IN 1894, WOMEN IN SOUTH AUSTRALIA were given the right to vote, and to stand for election to the parliament in that state. The Commonwealth of Australia, which came into being in 1901, established universal suffrage for all its citizens in 1902. Yet, when the LCA was constituted in 1966, women could not be delegates to LCA Synods, and were not given the right to vote in their local congregations in choosing the men who would represent their congregation. At a later date, the males in the congregation could, however, grant females the privilege of voting under certain conditions. In 1968, a resolution was adopted by the Synod meeting that women could be given the right to discuss and vote at meetings of the congregation provided that the principle was safeguarded that 'a woman is in subjection to man'. This would be demonstrated by 'recognising the right of the men to reserve the final decision on any matter to a male vote whenever the men desire to invoke this right'.[64]

A few years later, the 'Constitution for Congregations', prepared, endorsed and recommended for use in LCA congregations, made very clear that women do not enjoy the same status in the congregation as men. It spoke of membership as comprising baptised, confirmed and voting members and defined each in turn. Of voting members it stated:

> Voting members shall be confirmed members. The voting rights shall be defined in the By-laws. The right to vote may be granted to the women of the congregation, provided that the Scriptural principle contained in 1 Timothy 2:8-15 and related passages is respected.[65]

What is surprising is that there was no attempt made to define what was 'the principle contained in 1 Timothy 2:8-15 and related passages'.

Further reference was made to 'Scriptural principles' under the clause dealing with *Officers and Administration*:

> 3. The office of pastor, elder, chairman and lay-reader shall be restricted to male confirmed members in conformity with Scriptural principles.[66]

Just how determined the LCA was to make sure males were in control and that females were subordinate to them can be seen from the inclusion in the 'Model Constitution for Congregations' in a note appended to By-law Clause 1, defining voting membership:

> Where a congregation desires to do so, the following may be added at the appropriate place in By-law 1: Provided nevertheless that if it

is moved and seconded by two male voting members before any matter is voted on, that the matter shall be decided by the male voting members present, and if those male voting members first decide by a majority vote that the matter shall be so made by them, then the matter shall be decided at that meeting by a majority of those male voting members present.[67]

There must surely have been many within the LCA at the time who shared my feelings of shame and embarrassment that such recommendations and decisions should have been made and recorded for posterity in these official documents; it is salutary, nevertheless, to be reminded of these appalling official decisions and recommendations. For here one sees legalism at work, seeking to spell out in explicit detail an alleged principle, which the Model Constitution itself does not define, to ensure males remained in control. There can be no doubt that the passage mistakenly used to provide a justification for these decisions and recommendations was 1 Timothy 2:8-15. It is therefore imperative to discover if there was some Scriptural principle in the Timothy passage determining that males were to be in control in congregations. But since the voting rights of females is now recognised, the Scriptural principle (whatever it was a few decades earlier) is no longer in force! But it is clearly still in force in respect to women being excluded from the public ministry. For this is demanded in the Theses of Agreement, final paragraph of 'Theses VI. Theses on the Office the Ministry', where 1 Corinthians 14:34-35 and 1 Timothy 2:11-14 'prohibit a woman from being called into office of the public ministry...This apostolic rule is binding on all Christendom...'.[68] Before seeking to deal with the passage from 1 Timothy in an exegetical way, there are three issues that need to be raised in connection with this passage. The first deals with the matter of authorship.

The Authorship of the Pastorals

There are weighty reasons for questioning the authorship of Paul.[69] The external evidence in support of the Pauline authorship is not strong.[70] The fact that the writer of the Pastorals claims to be Paul and refers to personal details (especially in 2 Timothy) that would support Paul's authorship, does not, of course, assure its authenticity.[71] It is my view that the Pastorals contain genuine Pauline portions, but that the form in which the Pastorals have come to us is post-Pauline. The style of the Pastorals is unlike Galatians and Romans, where one is carried along by the argumentation. The Pastorals by comparison are piecemeal. Harris has pointed out that the method employed in dealing with the heretics in the Pastorals correspondence is in marked contrast with the method employed in genuine Pauline letters.[72] As we shall see in our consideration of 1 Timothy 2, there are real difficulties in ascribing this passage to Paul.

The Pastorals, furthermore, do not seem to fit into the church scene during Paul's lifetime, and a later date seems to be indicated.[73] In 1 Corinthians 7:8, he advised widows not to remarry, but in 1 Timothy 5:14, very different advice is given. In 1 Corinthians, the gifts of the Spirit are experienced in rich, almost tumultuous profusion; in the Pastorals the Spirit's gifts hardly rate a mention, with the writer determined to establish a highly structured form of church life and polity. In 2 Corinthians 11:30ff, Paul speaks of his sufferings in the world as almost a badge of honour; whereas in the Pastorals the stress is on peaceful coexistence with the world, and good citizenship as the ideal for Christians to strive after.[74] Quite clearly, the writer of the Pastorals is not expecting an imminent Parousia (which influenced Paul to give the advice he did in 1 Corinthians 7:26-31), but, like the writer of Acts, he has in mind the church's need to prepare and organise for an ongoing sojourn in the world.

While there are problems with Pauline authorship of the Pastorals, I am not questioning the importance of 1 Timothy's place in the New Testament canon. It is part of that body of writings which the church accepts as the authoritative Scriptures. Even if it could be clearly demonstrated that the Pastorals were not written by Paul, one would not be justified in excising them from the canon, nor even in dismissing their contents as unimportant for the church. They need to be treated with great respect as important writings from the early church, written by a person who was guided by the Spirit to write matters which were of considerable importance for the church in his time. What their significance is for the church of later generations is a question which must exercise the judgment of theologians in every age.

Background and Destination of 1 Timothy

Whilst the letter is addressed to Timothy and contains instructions and directions to this individual, it is equally concerned with the life of people under his pastoral care. The writer is particularly concerned about the conduct of those who held office in the congregations. It would be invaluable to have more precise knowledge of the congregations, and especially of the problems or heresies that they were encountering. We know what the situation was in the Galatian and Corinthian churches and can readily appreciate the nature and contents of the letters Paul addressed to them. But though we have some evidence in the Pastorals concerning the troubles these letters were meant to address, the evidence is by no means clear-cut. Hence it has been suggested that the Pastorals were dealing with early Gnosticism,[75] Proto-Montanism,[76] or a form of Judeo-Christian Gnosticism.[77] What is of particular importance for our consideration of 1 Timothy 2 is that women come in for special mention in a way that suggests their personal involvement in the trouble. Rules and regulations are given for widows and women deacons,[78] marriage and child-bearing are highly commended[79] and there are strong suggestions of woman's gullibility and susceptibility to error.[80]

Relationship to 1 Corinthians 14:33-35

The third issue has already been raised in the exegesis of 1 Corinthians 14:34-35. It is the assumption that these two passages are parallel statements by the same author, dealing with the same problems in two different letters. As will be demonstrated later, the writer of 1 Timothy is seeking to combat a form of false teaching in which certain women were involved; a form of teaching in which there was usurpation of authority over men. The Corinthian situation was of an altogether different kind.[81] Another difficulty for those who see the two passages in close correspondence is that the Corinthian passage has *lalein* (speak) and not *didaskein* (teach).The speaking to which the writer in 1 Corinthians is referring to is explained in v. 35 as wives wanting to know matters that they should find out from their husbands at home.

It has been claimed (in spite of the clear evidence shown above) that the consistency between the Corinthian and 1 Timothy passages gives added weight and authority to what Paul wrote.[82] If consistency is an important consideration, then there is a need to question the Pauline authorship of both passages, for they are inconsistent with Paul's clearly enunciated principle in Galatians 3 and the practice of Paul over against women in the early church.[83] Some indeed see a consistency between 1 Corinthians 14:34-35 and 1 Timothy 2, but regard both as non-Pauline. It is their contention that 1 Corinthians 14:34-35 was inserted into the text by a scribe who felt that if the Corinthian passage was thus inserted it would strengthen 1 Timothy 2.[84] There is no textual support for this. That would appear to be a 'way-out' claim to evade the issue. Rather than deleting the passage, how is it to be understood?

What is the Timothy Passage Saying in Its Context?

1 Timothy 2 clearly shows the writer's concern for responsible Christian citizenship and godly behaviour on the part of women and men in Timothy's congregations. Though the rules and instructions relate particularly to congregational order (*Gemeindetafeln*), they go beyond the worship situation and set forth appropriate conduct for daily life.[85] After the offering of prayers for all men (2:1ff), he turns his attention to the ways in which such prayer should be offered:

> I desire that in every place the men should pray,
> lifting up holy hands without anger or quarrelling;

also that women should adorn themselves modestly and sensibly in seeming apparel, not with braided hair or gold or pearls or costly apparel, but by good deeds, as befits women who profess religion (1 Timothy 2:8-10).

It is his desire (*boulamai*), not a command from the Lord, but his wish, that in every place (cf. Malachi 1:11) where they meet for worship and prayer, the men should pray with a peaceful disposition.[86] The lifting up of holy hands was the outward expression of people praying with sincerity and humility.[87] Uplifted hand was the stance used by Jews and Gentiles engaged in prayer, and there is evidence in the catacombs that was also the practice of Christians engaged in prayer.[88] Only the most determined literalist would insist that this is the stance one must adopt whilst praying today. Undoubtedly, what is vitally important is the instruction that men should pray without any angry, bitter thoughts and feelings.

The writer of 1 Timothy then turns his attention to the women.[89] It is necessary to complete the sentence by adding verbs from the previous sentence so that it would read, 'Likewise I desire that the women should pray....'[90] Just as the men should pray without quarrelling, so the women should pray modestly and appropriately dressed. He considers braided hair and the use of gold and pearls and costly clothing unbecoming for women engaged in prayer. Again, no one but the most determined literalist would insist that women should not wear jewellery or expensive dresses when attending worship services or prayer meetings in our day. Whilst some fundamentalist traditions apply this rule literally, most churches today would recognise that this is a matter of Christian freedom. A sizeable proportion of women in many congregations today would need to be sent home to change their clothes if these words were to be applied in a strictly literal way.

The principle that is valid for all time is that women taking part in worship ought to avoid all ostentation and immodesty in dress; their true ornamentation is not something external at all.[91] Had the writer lived at another age, he may well have not restricted this instruction to women, but would have included men who should dress without ostentation. Likewise, it would be equally appropriate to include women among the people who ought to pray without bitterness and anger. Likewise, the exhortation to good deeds (v. 10) belongs as much to men as to women. There are thus traces of sexual stereotyping in these verses that a writer with a higher degree of sensitivity in this area would want to avoid.

The Crucial Verses

We come now to the verses that have been used so repeatedly in LCA documents to exclude women from the office of ministry. They have been employed in such a way as to suggest that the writer of 1 Timothy was fully aware of the issues that would face the church in the 20th and 21st centuries, over against women's suffrage and women's part in the ministry – and he was implacably opposed to both!

In verses 11 and 12, the writer states further what he desires of women in regard to their conduct 'in every place', i.e. wherever people come together for prayer and worship:

> Let a woman/wife learn in silence with all submissiveness. I do not permit a woman/wife to

teach, nor to usurp authority over a man/husband; she is to be quiet.

The two words of crucial importance for a correct understanding of what the writer was addressing to Timothy are 'teach' (*didaskein*) and 'usurp authority' (*authentein*). *Didaskein* is found some 80 times in the four Gospels and in the Acts of the Apostles, but it occurs less frequently in the letters of Paul and the Pastorals. In Colossians 1:28 and 3:16, it is linked with *nouthetein* ('admonish'), and in 1 Timothy 4:11 with *parangellein* ('insist on'). In the Pauline letters, it is spoken of as a gift (*charisma*) not restricted to an appointed office in the church, but rather an activity and gift of the Spirit in which many may share in the worship life of the church (1 Corinthians 12:28f; Ephesians 4:11; 1 Corinthians 14:26ff; cf. James 3:1; Hebrews 5:12). Its use on the Pastorals suggests that the teaching, which earlier had been undertaken quite spontaneously by anyone who had the gift of the Spirit, is now regarded as a function exercised chiefly in the office of *episkopos* ('bishop' 1 Timothy 3:2) and of *presbyteros* ('elder' 5:17). Timothy is instructed as to what he is to teach, and he is also to make sure that others are also properly instructed, so that the right teaching is handed down (1 Timothy 2:7; 2 Timothy 1:11). There are pointed warnings against false teachers and different teachings (2 Timothy 4:3; Titus 1:9-11; 2:1; 1 Timothy 1:4; 6:3).[92]

Combating False Teachers

While there is a greater emphasis in the Pastorals on teaching as the special responsibility of persons in ecclesiastical office, it should be recognised that it was not restricted to such. It would seem that one of the ways the writer hopes to overcome the spread of false teaching, lies and godless chatter was to regulate and control more closely the teaching function in the congregations. If it is assumed that the Pastorals are all concerned with the same sort of errors troubling the congregations for which Timothy and Titus are responsible, it is possible to reconstruct the false teachings in broad outline. The errorists stressed ascetic practices and condemned marriage. The writer's response to this was to emphasise that marriage and raising a family are to be highly regarded by Christians (1 Timothy 4:1-4; 2:15; 5:14; Titus 2:4). Other aspects of the errors encountered in the congregations was a kind of spiritual enthusiasm and theological speculation that was disturbing the faith of some.

These aberrations were detrimental to good order in the congregations and were endangering the church's image in the world (1 Timothy 1:3-7; 2:2-3; 3:6-7; 6:1; etc). The writer provides specific instructions concerning the character and qualifications of those persons who should be appointed to office in the congregations as bishops, deacons, elders, widows (1 Timothy 3:1-14; 5:3-22; Titus 1:5-9); one of his special concerns is that through such persons sound doctrine may be proclaimed and the traditions maintained (1 Timothy 1:10; 2:7; 4:1,6,11;6:3; 2 Timothy 4:3; Titus 1:9-11; 2:1; 3:18ff). He reminds Timothy that the Scriptures are an important basis for teaching in the church (2 Timothy 3:14ff). A constantly recurring theme is the need for good deeds and blameless lives, and sound teaching should be directed to this end (1Timothy 2:8-10; 5:11-13; Titus 2:3-6; 2 Timothy 3:6-7, etc). Some of the comments the writer makes in respect to women convey negative overtones (1 Timothy 3:11; 5:11-13; Titus 2:3-6; 2 Timothy 3:6-7). Some women had obviously been deceived by heretical teachers and may have become false teachers themselves (Titus 1:11; 1 Timothy 5:15).

How 'Teaching' is Described

Against this background, the writer's instructions 'I do not permit a woman/wife to teach' is to be viewed. The sort of teaching that he does not permit a woman to engage in is spelled out in the following sentence: *oude authentein andros*. The key word is clearly *authentein*, but unfortunately it a rare word, found nowhere else in the New Testament, nor in the LXX, and only in a few places in secular literature. It does not receive a mention in Kittel's *Theological Dictionary of the New Testament*. Catherine Kroger, whilst pointing out that there has been virtually no 20th century scholarship concerning the meaning of this rare word, has established a strong argument in support of her contention that it means something more than to 'domineer'. She wrote:

> A survey of extra-biblical materials shows that it was not until the second or third century after Christ that the word came to have a sense of exercising mastery. The most common early usage of this rare word was to commit suicide, to murder another with one's own hands, or even to be a member of the murderer's family. By contrast it also meant to originate or to begin... The one early instance of a derivative word, which may imply rule or mastery, occurs in Euripides' Suppliants (lines 442-3), where it has a strongly sexual, indeed pederastic sense. A Rhodes scholar whom we consulted about

this passage complained that it was as dirty and coarse a Greek phrase that he had ever been called upon to translate. Euripides may also use the word particularly to signify a sexual verb whose subtleties escape us: 'sleeping with a man, *authetoon* to bear a child' (Andromache, 172). In the extended passage, lines 169-180, the concepts of eroticism and murder are intertwined. The word occurs again in an erotic sense in Trojan Women, (660). The ancient grammarians Phrynicus, Moeris, Pawcius and Thomas Magister advised against using this, or its derivatives and suggested a 'cleaner' verb instead... It appears to correspond to a modern four-letter word, and ancient Greece was replete with language of this type. We have then a verb which means both to kill and to originate, a word with strong erotic overtones, one with a double meaning. In the context of the Ephesian heresy, it might well mean to proselytise or hold a man in her sway through sexuality, or to perform a ritual murder in sexual practice in order that the initiate might be born again....[93]

N. J. Hommes has written:

The history of the word with respect to its origin as well as its shift in meaning is very remarkable... The noun *authentes* originally meant a suicide, a family murderer. As such it is found in a great many classic writers like Aeschylus, Sophocles, Herodotus, Thycidides and Euripides. In later times, it came to mean 'lord', 'master' 'autocrat'... It is believed that the word *authentes* was composed of *autos* and *entes*; this last word then having the significance of 'guilty'... Thus the original meaning would have been 'the one who is guilty over against himself, who puts his hand to himself.' Investigators have shown that the word comes from slang. Thus, the Atticist Thomas Magister admonishes his pupils to use *autodikein* instead of *authentein* since the last word is vulgar slang... From the significance of the word *autodikein*, which is a more decent synonym for *authentein* it is possible to shed some light on the question how the shift in meaning from 'suicide' to 'lord' has come about, for *autodikein* means to 'judge by one's own standards', 'to act on one's own authority', and thus 'to decide'. Someone who does this over against himself, makes a self-authorised move against himself, takes his life into his own hands. Whoever does this to someone else is dictatorial. From the foregoing it appears clearly now that the root-meaning of the word used by the writer in 1 Timothy 2:12 contains the element of 'guilty, self-willed, arbitrary behaviour'. Hence the author forbids in 1 Timothy 2:12 that 'teaching, i.e. discussing and admonishing which is the same as *authentein* over against the husband, i.e. arbitrary, conceited behaviour... The root meaning of *authentein*, therefore, has been well established: self-willed, arbitrary, interference in what is not properly one's domain, and thus trespassing the established limits.[94]

A Key Word

It is thus apparent that *authentein* in 1 Timothy 2 is an extremely strong word and was intended to convey something far more than our usual meaning of 'exercise authority over'. It is, therefore, totally unjustified to claim and teach, as the LCA has done for decades, that if women were to take part in synodical meetings, speak and vote at congregational meetings, exercise pastoral oversight and spiritual leadership in the office of pastor they would be guilty of the coarse, tyrannical conduct condemned by the strong verb *authentein*. The use of this word in the Theses of Agreement dealing with the ministry of Word and sacraments to exclude women from being ordained into this office strongly suggests that if a woman, properly qualified and duly called, were to preach a sermon or exercise some other element of pastoral ministry she would be behaving in a self-willed arbitrary, controlling manner over against the men and women who have called her into this office! To make such a claim seventy years ago and to repeat it decade after decade is surely a gross misuse of a passage which has been clearly misunderstood, misinterpreted and unfairly applied to women in ministry.

The writer of the letter to Timothy does not want wives to be engaged in the sort of teaching activity in the congregation that would mean acting in a tyrannical way in respect to their husbands. It would seem that what was happening in those congregations was that the women or wives, in the time of discussion and sharing in the service were 'tearing strips' off their husbands, instead of displaying the submission and quietness that was expected of wives in that society.

That women were not forbidden to teach, instruct and inform men in regard to God's will and saving purposes is clear from numerous examples of women, whose involvement in this work is recorded either without comment or in a way that suggests apostolic approval.[95] Clearly then the sort of teaching that the writer forbids wives/women to engage in must not be made so all embracing as to condemn also those women who were engaged in an altogether other form of teaching. He is concerned with a form of teaching in which wives act in an arbitrary, bossy, domineering way over against their husbands. Clearly then, one would need much better authority than the words in 1 Timothy 2 to contend that it is contrary to God's will for a woman to be a delegate at a church convention, to preach a sermon or serve as an elder or chairperson of a congregation, or to be a member of a policy-making board of the LCA, for the words in 1 Timothy strongly suggest an entirely different sort of activity.

The writer contrasts the attitude of quiet submissiveness with teaching that is dictatorial. It is his intention that women should learn with all submissiveness (*hypotage*) (verse 11). The submissiveness he expects of women has been explained as 'submission in the sense of renunciation of initiative'.[96] It is thus a further expansion of learning 'in silence'. Twice in these verses he insists on women being silent or quiet.[97] Instead of that teaching which he considers tyrannical, domineering activity, they should be quiet, they should learn with a submissive attitude.

Attention has already been drawn to the fact that there were numerous women in the early church who were engaged in teaching, praying, prophesying and witnessing, and thus were most certainly not silent. If one is to avoid a situation of having one passage of Scripture contradict and repudiate a practice which clearly had Christ's and Paul's approval, and if we are to take seriously the exceptionally strong word *authentein*, one is forced to the conclusion that the Timothy passage must have been directed to a specific problem encountered by Timothy in the congregations under his jurisdiction.

The Serious Problem in the Church

In an attempt to reconstruct the scene in Ephesus to which the letter is addressed, we face great difficulty because of uncertainty as to the time of writing. If it was a genuine Pauline letter, the date would be in the early 60s, but if it was not from Paul's hands the letter may have been written in the early part of the second century. One would need to know much more about church life in Ephesus (1 Timothy 1:3) during the period from 60 to 120 to speak with any authority, but from the evidence that we do have, it can be claimed that the church must have been having serious problems on account of heresy.

Ephesus was the capital of the Roman province of Asia and was on one of the main trade routes between Greece and Asia. It was the centre for a group of John's followers who spoke in tongues, and prophesied after receiving the Spirit through the laying on of hands (Acts 19:1-7). One of the results of Paul's ministry in the city was the burning of a large number of books on magic (Acts 19:19-20). A popular uprising was instigated by the silver-smiths against Paul when his preaching caused a marked falling off in trade for these business men (Acts 19:23ff). The seer in Revelation 2:1-7 warns the church against 'false apostles', and admonishes them for having 'abandoned the love they had at first, but commends them because they, like the seer, 'hate the works of the Nicolaitans'. This suggests they were being troubled by the

Nicolaitans, whom it seems ate food sacrificed to idols and practised immorality. Ephesus was famous in the ancient world for its temple of Diana, one of the ancient world's seven wonders. It has been claimed that cultic prostitution in the temple of Diana was organised along the lines of a beehive (the priestesses were named 'honeybees'), and for males to mate with them meant death.[98] If the letter to the Ephesians is considered to be appropriately addressed, there is a possible parallel between the 'empty words' of Ephesians 5:6 and the 'godless chatter of the Pastorals' (1 Timothy 6:20; 2 Timothy 2:16).

In such a situation, it is not difficult to understand the demand that women should be silent rather than continuing to expound their views in the assembly – a practice that the writer considered domineering behaviour over their husbands. Given his concern for good order, the church's image in the community, the importance of proven leaders, and bearing in mind the social norms of the day in respect to women's role in society and their submission to their husbands, the writer was determined to pull these women into line. He insists on a form of behaviour in the congregation that would achieve these objectives. Massingberd Ford contended that in the second century the Montanist heresy had its beginnings in the region to which the Pastorals were addressed, and it was known as the Cataphrygian or Phrygian heresy. She contended that the Pastorals were directed to an early form of this error, Proto-Montanism. Women played an important part in this movement. Maximilla and Priscilla were accused of paying heed to deceitful spirits, of being inspired by the devil. Fasting was insisted on: 'The Montanist women apparently taught in the community, prophesied falsely, left their husbands... became bishops and priests'.[99]

Dibelius and Conzelmann contended:

> The motivation and objectives of this extensive treatment to the questions relating to women are to be sought in the situation in the congregations which the author had in mind. The commandment to silence during the assembly of the congregation was explained by Theodoret (III,650 Schulze) this way: Since women too have the gift of prophetic speech, it was necessary that he give instructions also about that... That within the scope of Paul's mission it was possible for women to teach is shown in Acts 18:16. In Gnostic circles, individual virgins had privileged positions. 2 Timothy 3:6 shows that women played some kind of a role among the opponents of the Pastoral letters. The *Acts of Paul* also provide material on this question. To be sure, their relationship to the Pastorals is a matter of controversy. But it seems likely that they point to movements similar to those which must be presupposed for the context of our author, and especially to his opponents. The position which Thekla assumes in the *Acts of Paul* as teacher and preacher is very relevant to this context. But Gnostic or semi-Gnostic ideas could also provide the background for the positive mention of child-bearing in 1 Timothy...[100]

1 Timothy fits very naturally into this sort of situation, in which the author was dealing with an outbreak of undisciplined charismatic emancipation. This caused the

church to be in danger of losing the sound doctrine and good order that were so important. The sort of troubles, which the church in the second century experienced, were probably already causing problems in the congregations for which Timothy was responsible. Hence the instructions to Timothy to take the action the letter spells out.

How Valid are the Reasons for Not Teaching?

We come now to the reasons the writer advances in support of his contention that wives must not teach, but learn in silence, and not domineer over their husbands:

> For Adam was formed first, then Eve; and Adam was not deceived, but the woman was deceived and became a transgressor (13-14).

There are two arguments advanced here in support of the writer's view that women should learn quietly and not teach and exercise authority over their husbands – the priority of Adam and the gullibility of the women. It is not without ample justification that these arguments are considered unconvincing.[101] The writer is suggesting that because Adam was created ahead of the woman, this priority in time gives him superiority over the woman, and makes him a more fit and competent person to teach than the one who is later in time. He implies that the one who came later was less competent or less qualified than that which preceded her.[102]

The arguments the writer advances are full of illogical and seriously questionable statements, and can be readily dismissed. For example: i) Animals were created before Adam, does that make them superior to man? John the Baptist was ahead of Jesus, but that does not make him superior to Mary's son; ii) In the creation story in Genesis 1, both male and female are created in God's image and both are instructed to exercise authority over the whole of creation. There is no suggestion that one has greater authority than the other; iii) In the second creation story in Genesis 2 where the focus is on marriage, there is no suggestion that being created second 'out of Adam's rib', implies that she is in any respect less than her husband or that an order to superiority and inferiority was being established; iv) The implication that women are inherently gullible and unstable because Eve was deceived, and therefore women must not teach, is unconvincing to say the least. Hanson was undoubtedly fully justified in his comment: 'The author of the Pastorals nowhere shows his theological inferiority to Paul more clearly than in this passage.'[103] The quality and theological standard of the writer is not improved by his next verse:

> Yet woman will be saved through child-bearing if she continues in faith and love and holiness, with modesty (v. 15).

However favourably and charitably one seeks to interpret 1 Timothy 2:13-15, these verses seem to be far removed from the sort of theology one expects from a writer like Paul. There is no hint of the gospel, no word of the liberation and freedom men and women have by faith in Christ, no suggestion concerning oneness and life in the Spirit, no reference to the new order of things brought into being through the resurrection of Jesus Christ, no mention of baptism, no appeal to his readers to respond out of gratitude for what God had done for them and in them, no offer of hope in view of the nearness of the end. These are all characteristic themes of Paul for which we look in vain in this pericope.

Instead the writer shows close affinity to assorted parenthetic and rabbinic teachings. Dibelius and Conzelmann drew attention to the following parallels. In regard to the way godly women are expected to adorn themselves (vs 9f): Regulations concerning clothing in the great mystery inscriptions of Andania (Ditt.Sy11.11 736,15ff., esp. 22f) have this to say about the 'holy women' (*ierai gynaikes*): 'She must not wear any gold ornament, nor put rouge, nor white paint, nor a wreath, nor braid her hair, nor put on shoes; but she should only wear clothes of felt or skins of sacrificial animals'.[104] Concerning the directions that wives should be quiet, in subjection to their husband, not teach, or act in a domineering way toward them (2:11-12), the same writers refer to a fragment from the comedian Philemon: 'It is a good wife's duty, O Nikostrate, to be devoted to her husband, but in subordination; a wife who prevails is a great evil'.[105]

The writer to Timothy, in arguing that Eve was deceived, but Adam was not, and therefore women are not to teach, is reflecting the commonly held view that women were less stable than men. Hanson has pointed out that:

> ... in Jewish tradition before the time of Paul women were regarded as both inferior to men because created later, and naturally more gullible than men, two points made by the writer to Timothy... As for gullibility this meets us as early as the letter to Aristeas, where it is said of women that they 'easily change their minds as a result of a specious argument'. Similarly, Philo, discussing why the serpent speaks to the woman and not to the man, writes: 'And the woman is more accustomed to being deceived than man. For his judgment, like his body is masculine and

is capable of dissolving or destroying the designs of deception; but the judgment of the woman is more feminine and because of softness she easily gives way and is taken in by plausible falsehoods which resemble the truth'.[106]

The notion that Eve was deceived (*exapatetheisa*) in the sense of 'sexually seduced' is clearly implied in 4 Maccabees 18:6-8:

> I was a pure maiden and I strayed not from my father's house, and I kept guard over the rib that was built into Eve. No seducer of the desert, no deceiver of the field corrupted me; nor did the false beguiling serpent sully the purity of my maidenhood.

First Century Jewish Influences

It has thus been shown that the writer of 1 Timothy, in support for his views concerning women in the church and society, uses arguments and interpretations that were prevalent among Jews in the first century. The fact that he uses such arguments as a basis for conclusions and principles, which are not drawn elsewhere in Scripture on the basis of the same Old Testament narratives, ought to make us wary, to say the least, of regarding the principles he is trying to establish as forever valid. No other passage in the New Testament suggests that woman is inferior to man because Eve was deceived but Adam was not, therefore making woman unsuitable to teach.

The writer's way of doing exegesis reflects clearly the culture of the time and the androcentric attitudes prevailing towards women. But we are not living in that culture. It is fortunately not the popular belief in our society that women are inferior to men because Adam was created ahead of Eve! Here and there, the sexist myth may still prevail that women are more gullible than men, but if it is expressed it would rightly and quickly be denounced. How then does this passage apply to our society and the church in this culture? There have been those who maintained that 1 Timothy 2 established a principle that women in the church are to be in subjection to men, and for this reason they do not have voting rights in the congregation. The principle allegedly contained in 1 Timothy 2 was also seen to have application in the 20th century in preventing women from serving in their congregations as elders, lay readers, lay-preachers and chairpersons, for in such positions they would be teaching and having authority over men. Even now the passage is still seen as establishing a principle, 'binding on all Christendom', that women must not be called into the public ministry of the church.

Need to Review and Discard

The exegesis has raised serious questions as to whether such principles are in fact contained in 1 Timothy 2. It has also raised serious doubts as to whether it is theologically valid to make a rule for the church today from the interpretation and application made by a biblical writer from totally different circumstances. It is my firm conviction that the applications made in the LCA over the past seventy years in respect to the Timothy passage need to be revised and rejected. I submit the following summary statements as reasons for a reconsideration of the validity of the applications the LCA has made on the basis of 1 Timothy 2:8-15:

1. The passage in its totality is culturally orientated. It deals with proper stance and attitude of men when praying, the proper dress for women who pray in church, and the wife in subjection to her husband.
2. It is totally inconsistent that one of the pieces of instruction ('women must not teach') is to be applied in a literal sense, so that they may not preach or teach in the church's public ministry, whereas other pieces of the same instruction ('lifting up holy hands...' 'not with braided hair or gold or pearls or costly attire') are not applied literally.
3. It is directed to a specific situation to a person who had responsibility for dealing with the particular problem. The situation facing the church today, whether women may or may not be called in the public ministry in no way resembles what Timothy was facing.
4. The key word *authentein* in no way describes the sort of activity that a woman graduate from a theological seminary and duly called by the church would be guilty of in undertaking the work of a pastor.
5. The writer of 1 Timothy is concerned about wives in relationship to their husbands, not women over against men as in the present dispute re women's ordination.
6. The reasons given in support of the writer's instructions are not grounded in the gospel, but based on an interpretation of creation and fall stories popular in rabbinic theology.
7. There is no clear parallel to this prohibition regarding women in any other New Testament passage. 1 Corinthians 14:34-35 deals with an altogether different situation.

8. If the Timothy passage is applied so as to prevent women from being called to share with men in the responsibilities of the pastoral office, it is being given greater normative value for the church today than those passages in the New Testament that speak of women sharing in the same ministries as men in the New Testament churches.
9. If it is taught that the principle stated in 1 Timothy 2:11-12 applies today to prevent women from holding all such offices where they might have authority over men in the church, then the reasons that the writer gives to support his ruling ought to be also presented, namely, Adam had priority over Eve, it was the woman, not her husband who was deceived and fell into sin, and woman's proper role is child-bearing!
10. If women may not teach men or hold positions of responsibility and authority in the church, because women are more likely to be deceived than men and lead men into error, then logic would surely demand that women be removed from teaching in church schools and Sunday schools, where they teach unsuspecting children. Surely, it is much more urgent to protect trusting innocent children than their more astute fathers and uncles!
11. The writer of 1 Timothy considered the proper function of women was to bear children. In his time, it was presumably a life-long task: it is not so in our day. Marrying and child-rearing need not preclude a woman from engaging in other tasks and responsibilities outside the home. The current New Zealand Prime Minister, Jacinda Ardern, has coped wonderfully well with child-rearing and being a country's Prime Minister; likewise, dozens of female ministers in the Uniting Church in Australia combine ministry with family responsibilities.

Incidentally, the writer of 1 Timothy does not address the issue of some women choosing not to marry, and others cannot or choose not to produce children.

Given the difficulties in the passage itself, the uncertainties surrounding its destination, and the obvious influence on the writer from his social, religious and cultural background, its total lack of support from other New Testament passages, it is more than unwise, it is a serious mistake to try to establish and insist on maintaining a doctrine and practice based on such a text. By maintaining this misguided teaching the church is also saying that this one text is of enduring normative importance, whereas Galatians 3:26-29 and 1 Corinthians 11:5 and the practice in the Pauline churches where women shared in the important aspects of ministry, are not important or not relevant to the present situation.

If, as Oscar Cullman claimed: 'The fountain head of all false biblical interpretation and all heresy is invariably the isolation and absolutizing of one single passage',[107] it is incumbent upon the church in the 21st century to re-examine and correct its long-held mistaken position on this matter.

Chapter 5

Creation and Fall Narratives
Genesis 1:26-28; 2:4-24; 3:1-21

IT IS MY CONTENTION THAT THE CREATION NARRATIVES (Genesis 1 and 2) do not provide theological support for the theory of woman's subordination to man; instead, in these chapters man and woman are presented in complementary roles, both in God's image, in a relationship of shared responsibility and mutuality. This relationship was, however, shattered by the fall into sin, and one of the resultant evils was the husband's domination of his wife. The consequence for Eve of the curse of sin, as for her husband, are descriptive rather than prescriptive. It is, furthermore, my contention that Jesus Christ, the woman's seed, has come to bring freedom from the curse of sin and to restore the shattered relationships that resulted from humankind's disobedience. Consequently, to regard the statement 'he shall rule over you' as prescriptive for woman's relationship with man for all time would be as foolish as to insist that the curse resting on man ('thorns and thistles') must be experienced in full every day.

At the time of the formation of the LCA, the theologians of both churches saw in the early chapters of Genesis support for the notion that woman is subordinate to man. The Joint

Faculties of Concordia and Immanuel Seminaries were asked for an opinion on whether women ought to be entitled to vote in the congregations of the new church (LCA). A Statement was prepared and adopted by the combined Church Councils of the amalgamating churches in 1966. It clearly emphasised the subordination of women to men, claiming that the creation and fall narratives of Genesis support this teaching:

1. In Christ man and woman have equal standing, Mark 12:36 and parallels, Galatians 3:28; but there is a difference between man and woman by virtue of the fact of creation, 1 Corinthians 11:7-10; 1 Timothy 2:13; Genesis 2:18ff, by which a subordinate position has been given to woman. A further reason is the role played by woman at the fall, Genesis 3:1ff; 1 Timothy 2:14.This subordination shows itself, as far as the individual woman is concerned in the marriage relationship Genesis 3:16.
2. This difference between man and woman, traceable back to creation and the fall, is not set aside in the Christian church as it exists on earth, where it is subject to all the ordinances of creation, 1 Corinthians 11:3,10; Ephesians 5:21f; Col. 3:18; 1 Peter 3:5ff.[108]

For more than a decade, this Statement was incorrectly promoted as having been 'Adopted by the Constituting Convention, 1966'. At the 1978 Convention of the LCA, the issue of women serving as delegates to national conventions was again debated. No decision was reached and a Statement prepared by the Commission on Theology and Church Relations (CTICR) was referred to state conventions for their consideration. What is of more than passing interest to me was the omission from the Statement of any reference to creation and fall narratives, which figure so prominently in previous statements dealing with women's voting rights at congregational meetings. So, progress was being made at last!

In 1979, the CTICR produced another statement which showed that the CTICR was divided over the interpretation and applicability of the creation and fall narratives in respect to woman's subordination to man. The compliers of the 'Pro' position (i.e. in favour of women being elected as delegates to conventions) omit any reference to Genesis 2 as providing a basis for subordination. They stated 'Paul never quotes Genesis 3:16 which says that after the fall the woman is be ruled by man. Such ruling is not part of life in the restored people of God. But those who opposed women being chosen as delegates to conventions still made use of Genesis 2:18ff to support their view that it was the Creator's design and purpose that woman be in subordination to man, with the fall into sin making the subordination harsh and painful'.[109]

Since the LCA has not acknowledged that it was mistaken when it claimed for decades that the notion of woman being subordinate to man was taught in the creation narratives, and since it is highly likely that such a mistaken notion is still held by some pastors and laypersons in the LCA, it is necessary to summarise how mistaken such claims are. It needs to be pointed out that though throughout Jewish history woman's status was presented as inferior to man's, the creation narratives do not contain the slightest trace of such social attitudes towards women.[110]

The Creation Story in Genesis 1

Phyllis Bird spoke of the creation of male and female in Genesis 1:26-28 as 'eloquent and enigmatic in its terseness'.[111]

It is also very beautiful. The creation of man (*'adham* = human-kind) is presented as the high point of the creation saga. After first declaring the divine intention to create humankind, describing and defining the unique relationship such creatures will have with their Creator ('in our image, after our likeness'), the Creator decrees that humankind is to have authority over the whole of creation. His intentions and plans are declared, then the action follows – humankind is created in God's image – male and female. As male and female, humankind is in relationship to one another, but also to God. As male and female, humankind's primary bond is with its Creator, not with the other creatures over which it is to have dominion. Humankind is thus created in relationships.[112] As male and female, they can hear God, love God, trust God and respond to him fully. As male and female, they exercise authority on behalf of God over the whole of the perfect creation. As male and female, they share in the ongoing work of creation (procreation). Thus, as male and female, they stand together, beneath God, different in their sexuality, but one (*'adham*), in a relationship of shared responsibility and of complete equality.

The Creation Story in Genesis 2

The relationship between the creation account in Genesis 1 and the second account in Genesis 2 must lie outside the scope of the present study. I regard the creation of man and woman in the Genesis 2 story as a filling out and an expansion of the earlier chapter. Again, the picture that emerges, clearly and strongly, is that God's glorious creation is complete only with the creation of humankind; man and woman stand over

Creation and Fall narratives

against God and one another in a special relationship, peculiar to them alone.

However, it is of some importance to note the way the writer stresses the significance of the woman's creation. The fact that the woman's creation is recorded at all is in itself remarkable, since this is, as Bailey has claimed, the 'only account of the creation of woman as such in Near Eastern literature'. But, in addition to that, whereas man's creation is described in one verse (v. 7), 'the woman's creation comes (v. 22) with man's response to it (v. 23) as the climax of verses 18-22, and indeed of the whole account of creation; she is the crown of creation'.[113] A feature of the Genesis 2 story is that the writer begins with man's creation, moves to the creation of Eden and the animals, and then, concludes with the creation of Eve. Trible termed this a 'ring composition' whereby the last mentioned completes the circle, and thus first and last stand together and are parallel to each other'.[114]

Man (*'adham*) is formed from the dust of the ground (*'adhamah*) v. 7. Man is both genus and an individual in this verse. He is from the ground, but when animated by the breath of God he becomes a living being, a psycho-physical self. But he is not yet complete because he stands alone. It is only with the creation of woman does *'adham* become *'ish*, a sexual and social being.[115]

The writer draws attention to the man's incompleteness and thus the incompleteness of the whole creation, by having God declare 'It is not good that the man should be alone' (v. 18). Aloneness was man's primary helplessness, his greatest need. The beasts of the field do not fulfil man's need for a helper/partner and cannot take away his loneliness and incompleteness. They cannot stand by his side, they are under his feet.[116] Only a woman created (built: *banah*) from man's side can give completeness and perfection to God's creation.

'A helper fit for him' does not mean a servant for man, but a person opposite to, yet corresponding to man. 'A helper like man, suited to man, worthy of man, corresponding to him' was Cassute's literal translation of the text.[117] The expression 'a helper fit for him'(*'ezer*) was seen by some to express a subordinate relationship of the woman in respect to man but there is no justification for this in the actual words used.[118] Trible has commented:

> In the Old Testament the word 'helper' (*'ezer*) has many usages. In our story it describes the animals and the woman... It is a relational term; it designates a beneficial relationship; and it pertains to God, people and animals. By itself the word does not infer inferiority. Position results from additional content or from the context. Accordingly, what kind of a relationship does *'ezer* infer in Genesis 2:18, 20? Our answer comes in two ways: 1) The word *neged*, which joins *'ezer*, connotes equality, a helper who is a counterpart. 2) The animals are helpers but they fail to fit *'adham*. There is physical, perhaps psychic, rapport between *'adham* and the animals, for Yahweh forms (*yasar*) them both from the ground (*'adhamah*). Yet their similarity is not equality. *'Adham* names them and thereby exercises power over them. No fit helper is among them. And thus, the narrative moves to woman. My translation is this: God is the helper superior to man; the animals are helpers inferior to man; woman is the helper equal to man.[119]

Genesis 2 highlights the fact that God is the creator of both the man and the woman. Man has no part in woman's creation – he is completely oblivious to what is happening, for the Lord has caused a deep sleep to fall on him. 'He is neither participant, nor spectator, nor consultant at her birth. Like man, woman owes her life solely to God. For both of them the origin of life is a divine mystery'.[120]

The building of the woman from the rib (or side) of the man suggests a common origin for man and woman. The fact that one is from the ground and the other is from the man does not suggest that one is superior to the other, but both owe their being entirely to God's creative power. Though woman is derived from man, she is not inferior for that reason, just as man is not inferior to the ground from which his body was formed by the Creator. Man and woman share in an essential identity – a fact that the man expresses when God brings the woman to the awakened man:

> This at last is bone of my bone and flesh of my flesh. She shall be called woman ('ishshah) because she was taken out of man ('ish) (v. 23).

'Adham had looked in vain among the animals for a helper fit for him, but now his searching is over for God brings to him the one whom he immediately recognises as a fellow creature, of the same nature but of a different sex. In fact, it is only now that he becomes aware of his own sexuality. Only now is 'adham truly 'ish. Man, as male, does not precede woman as female, but happens concurrently with her.[121] Only with the creation of 'ishshah is 'adham designated as 'ish.' By using the expression 'ishshah me'ish, which calls attention to the striking similarity between the Hebrew words for 'man' and 'woman', does the narrator seem to want to express the identity of the nature of, and the 'equality' of man and woman.'[122]

When the man designates the creature before him as woman, he is not naming her (as he named the animals and thereby established supremacy over them). 'Woman' is not a name, but a common noun, it designates gender not a person. What the writer is wanting to convey is that the man gladly accepts her as one who is worthy of being called by the same name as he had, and he joyfully acknowledges the equality of the partnership God has established between *'ish* and *'ishashah*. It is only after the fall that Adam called his wife's name Eve.

Thus, the Genesis 2 narrative highlights the creation of woman – the one like man without whom man is incomplete. Their essential oneness is proclaimed by the man. Their creation as social sexual persons are a doxology in honour of their Creator. Their sexuality is not primarily for procreation (as in Genesis 1:28), but is an essential expression of their completeness in each other. As man and woman, they are created for each other, to complete each other. Accordingly, their union in each other is a reunion.[123]

How it is possible to find, in the creation narratives, support for the notion of woman's subordination to man is extremely difficult for me to comprehend. Perhaps those who held that point of view assumed it was there and accordingly read the false notion into the ancient text. In only one respect does man have a distinction not enjoyed by woman. *'Adham* is created first. This does not imply that he therefore is in a position of rank or of superiority over the woman who came into existence later. What comes last in the created order of things is not inferior to what preceded it. God's new covenant is superior to the first, just as Christ's priesthood and sacrifice is superior to the Jewish system which preceded it (Hebrews 7-9).[124] God fashions both and gives them to each other as soul partners, sharing a common identity, origin and purpose.

The Fall into Sin and the Curse – Genesis 3:1-21

The joy and unity of the original relationship between man and woman is shattered by the disobedience of God's creatures. Genesis 3 gives prominence to the part played by the woman in the fall without, however, suggesting a greater degree of vulnerability or guilt on her part. The rest of the Old Testament Scriptures pass over her part in the fall in complete silence.[125] The woman is the one approached by the serpent and becomes engaged in theological discussion with the tempter. There is no reference to the man and no suggestion that it was improper for the woman to so occupy herself without her husband.[126] She desires the forbidden fruit and takes it, mistakenly believing that this is the way to real wisdom. She then gives some to her husband and he accepts it without question or protest of any kind. There is no support for the notion that, being more subtle than the other animals, the serpent recognised that the woman was more likely to yield to its deceptions than the man. On what grounds could it be argued that woman was less stable or more likely to be deceived than man? One might argue just as subjectively (and invalidly) that the serpent tempted the woman as the stronger of the two, realising that if there was success with her, then the man would blindly and rather stupidly follow the woman.

The Genesis narrative does not reflect on the reasons for the tempter's strategies. The woman was approached, she was deceived and disobeyed God's command. Whereas the woman engaged in theological debate, the man simply took what he was offered and ate. 'His one act is belly-oriented, and is an act of quiescence, not of initiative. The man is not dominant, he is not aggressive, he is not a decision-maker – he follows his wife without question and without comment and thereby denies his own individuality.'[127]

The prominence given to the woman in the fall narrative is continued in the section dealing with the pronouncement of judgment (3:14-19). It is the woman's offspring that will be engaged in conflict with the serpent's offspring, and the woman herself will experience great pain in her unique role of child-bearing. Her relationship with her husband will also experience conflict and pain 'for he shall rule over you'. Whereas the serpent is cursed, no curse is pronounced on the woman, nor on her husband. Adam finds that the ground is cursed, but not he himself. For Adam, there will now be thorns and thistles and the struggle of earning his daily bread in the face of hardships and disappointments; for his wife there will be the pain of child-bearing and the experience of being dominated by her husband, whereas previously she had been at his side, a co-partner with him in caring for God's creation. Their equality as man and woman and their union in one flesh would be impaired by the fact that her husband would now become also her lord.[128]

The punishments or judgments that came upon man and woman were thus descriptions of the sufferings and pain experienced by men and women in Hebrew society. Marriage and child-bearing were considered woman's primary role, and tilling the soil and supporting one's family were for man his primary task and responsibility.[129] In discharging these responsibilities, women and men experienced alienation, hardships and eventually death: In the most common and basic of tasks and relationships men and women would never be able to forget that their lives were lived after the fall.

Male Dominance over Females

The statement of particular importance is the word to the woman that her husband 'shall rule over' her. It is clearly not feasible to see this as a mandate for male dominance over females. It is an explanation for what was simply taken for granted in Jewish society. It was not a normative thing prescribing how it must be for men and women for all time, but a description of what happened when God's perfect creation went off the rails.[130] One of the tragic consequences was that partnership and equality were replaced by dominance and subordination. These were no more part of the Creator's plan than thorns, thistles, and eventual death – all perversions of the perfect order.

If it is claimed that the subordination of women to men is part of the divine order of things, then a consequence of the fall into sin is made normative, for as has been shown there is no suggestion in the creation narratives that woman is subordinate to man. This appears only after the fall into sin and is one of the consequences. If it is claimed that subordination is part of the divine order, then one dare not change it. But since it is in a context that speaks of the pain of childbirth (and thorns and thistle for men), these need to be regarded in the same way. These consequences too must also be regarded as normative. Hence it would be tampering with the divine order to provide pain-easing drugs and medication in childbirth, just as it would be opposing the divine order to provide herbicides, fertilisers and advanced food production for the farmer. Furthermore, if God intended that women must be subordinate to men, there dare not be any exceptions to this rule. If it belongs to the so-called orders of creation, it must be insisted on in the created order (not just in the church). Hence it would be contrary to the divine order of things for women to be in positions of authority over men in any walk of life. If the divine order is subordination, there would have to be opposition to female prime ministers, female monarchs, female judges, women in any position of authority and leadership over men in business, commerce, law and education.[131]

It would seem to be one of the major emphases of the creation and fall narratives in Genesis to highlight the contrast between the ideal state and the fallen state in the relationships people have with God, with one another and with the creation generally. To combine creation and fall narratives as though they were one in the matter of subordination demonstrates insufficient attention to the actual texts and the writer's purposes. Subordination was part of the punishment that has come upon women, just as man's life was afflicted with painful consequences resulting from the fall into sin. To insist on subordination, as was done in the LCA as an order of creation, is a serious mistake, for subordination is a consequence of an imperfect order of things. The male-female model portrayed in Genesis 3:16 is a model of disorder.[132]

In the teaching of our Lord, there is a very significant comment on marriage and divorce, which illustrates the point being stressed, namely, that there is sharp contrast between God's original creation and the fallen world, and that the disorder that prevailed in the fallen world was not mandatory. Jesus was questioned on the right of a man to divorce his wife (Matthew 19:3-9; Mark 10:2-12), and his reply contrasts the divorce legislation then prevalent with the original intention and plan of God. Divorce laws were established for the benefit of men and were an expression of male dominance ('hardness of heart'), which was a rejection of the equality and mutuality described in the creation stories. Jesus' understanding of sexuality and husband-wife relationships was based on key elements from Genesis 1:27 and 2:24, and he clearly repudiated the practice of divorce for which justification was found in the wife's subordination to a man. For him God had joined together two equal partners as one, thereby ruling out not only the male's prerogative of divorce (which Moses had sanctioned), but other forms of unfaithfulness by either party, which would weaken the marriage bond. Indeed, in the sermon on the mount he declared the sexuality to be so sacred that it must not be even secretly exploited from a distance by means of a lustful look (Matthew 5:27-28).[133]

The question that needed to be asked and grappled with in the LCA was, and still is, this: should woman's relationship with man be viewed from within the context of the original creation or from the context of the fall? In the present study of Galatians 3:26-31, an attempt was made to demonstrate that the redemptive work of Jesus has initiated a new order in which the old antagonism and rivalries so terribly real under the old order are to cease their destructive and divisive ways.[134] An important first step was taken for humankind by Jesus Christ to re-establish the unity and harmony God planned and initiated for humankind. Since in the bell-lap of world history, the old order and the new order exist side by side, tension and conflict are inevitable. Men and women redeemed by Christ will not always regard and treat each other as equals before God and in the world. This is the sad reality of life in the world where the curse of sin is forever real. But the church, God's new humanity, needs to exercise great determination in ensuring that it sees man and woman in accord with God's new order of things. Subordination was not part of an order of creation. Therefore, the church, the new creation, ought not to insist on it.

Shall we revert once more to the old order as if women had not been punished enough, and insist on keeping them in subjection, by refusing to accept them into the ordained ministry of the church? Or shall we take seriously the fact that Christ has come and liberated both male and female from their age-long strife to new possibilities of equality and mutual respect and caring?[135]

Chapter 6

Hermeneutical Presuppositions

THROUGHOUT THESE STUDIES, I have been grappling with questions related to the use that the church of today makes of directions and rules in Scripture based on very different social and cultural contexts. We are not the people addressed in the letters to the Galatians, Corinthians or to Timothy. Though it certainly was God's word to them, what is God's word to us for the issues and questions we have in regard to male-female relationships in church and society? Can we assume that the interpretation and application that these Scriptures had for them is the same interpretation and application that is has for us today?

Readers who have persevered to this point will be fully aware of the principles of biblical exegesis, which have been followed in this book. The reader will have formed judgments already about the validity of my hermeneutics. Though this chapter may be regarded by some as redundant, there may be value in restating in summary form some of the principles of biblical exegesis that I have considered especially important, and in drawing attention to one particular focus, which is of the utmost relevance for the matters under consideration.

Before taking up this 'Then and there: Here and now' focus in more detail, the following basic principles are restated:

1. The Scriptures of the Old and New Testaments are the inspired and authoritative Word of God.
2. The prime purpose of God in causing these Scriptures to be written and preserved for our day was to disclose the saving plans and purposes for the world through the eternal Son, our Lord Jesus Christ, the Word made flesh.
3. Since we are dealing with the revelation of a gracious God to sinful men and women, it is with considerable awe and profound respect that we need to approach these writings, and seek to understand their message for our lives.[136]
4. Such reverence does not preclude the need to submit the Scriptures to careful and respectful study and searching analysis, while at the same time letting the Scriptures interpret the Scriptures, and viewing the Old in the light of the New Testament.
5. Included in the searching analysis are such considerations as: meanings of words, syntax, context, author, purpose of writing and style of composition.
6. It is inevitable that the student of Scripture will bring to the text their own presuppositions, shaped by their culture, and their personal values and religious beliefs.
7. All the teachings and religious practices drawn from the Scriptures (the ultimate norm and basis for all doctrines and practices in the church) must be viewed from the perspective of the 'chief article of Christian doctrine' (*Augsburg Confession*, Article 28, par. 65-66): justification by grace alone, through faith in Jesus Christ.
8. Within the remarkable unity of the Scriptures, written over many hundreds of years, that is, the disclosing of a gracious God revealed in Jesus Christ, there is also

diversity. It is neither necessary nor possible to always demonstrate complete harmonisation and consistency.
9. The writers of Scripture wrote out of their historical and cultural setting. Though inspired by the Holy Spirit, so that their writings are truthful and trustworthy, they describe, reflect on and respond to the world as they knew it. In describing social conditions, they present them in their fallen state and illustrate the effect this has on every relationship.
10. The New Testament also emphasises the breaking in of God's new order with the incarnation, life, death and resurrection of Jesus Christ. His intervention has resulted in a new community, which continues to live in the old order, yet is freed from the curse and control of sin.
11. Not all of Scripture is equally normative. There are various levels of importance and applicability. There is much historical data and many rules and regulations that were part of the history of Old Testament times. The saving work of Christ in all its dimensions for human life is of primary importance.
12. The Scriptures have not given a single blueprint for church polity, congregational life and ministry. Such instructions as are given reflect the social, cultural and religious conditions of the day and place.
13. Only through the enlightenment of the Holy Spirit is it possible to understand the Scriptures and their application for the life of the church today. The Spirit makes possible a progressive awareness of scriptural truth. The church needs to be guided by the Holy Spirit in understanding Scripture. It also needs to recognise the influence of its own cultural setting, and take due account of the insights of scholarship, science, history, psychology and such like.

At no period of church history can it be claimed that the full and complete meaning of Scripture for all time has been disclosed.

Then and There: Here and Now

The Scriptures have come to us out of particular times and places. The persons, who were inspired by the Holy Spirit to write the books, now part of the Bible, lived within specific historical, social and religious contexts. They ate certain foods, thought along certain lines, believed certain things, held to certain values, followed certain rules and interpreted their religious experiences along certain lines. The men called by God to the task of writing gospels, letters or apocalypses brought to their task their individual backgrounds, education, style of writing, and all the other individualities and peculiarities induced by time, surroundings, mood, outlook and knowledge. They were fallible human beings.

Their writings were in certain literary forms. They were addressed to and intended for people and situations and places, usually to meet specific needs in the life of the people at that point in time. The church in every age in seeking to interpret and apply those writings has to pay attention to the literary form the writers employed, the purpose of their writing, the situation and culture out of which they wrote, and the way people thought then, felt and expressed themselves. If one, for example, looks at the stories and statements about women in the Bible, it is important to recognise that the writers are writing about people in their current historical and cultural settings, and it is inevitable that they would reflect the sort of perspectives their culture had over against women.

Now whilst they operated from a setting in which there were certain presuppositions over against women, the inspired writers did not always stay within such norms. As was shown earlier, Paul demonstrated that the gospel of Christ has had revolutionary impact on male-female relationships. Paul's theological initiative expressed in Galatians 3:28 and in 1 Corinthians 11:1-2, as the counterbalance to 11:8-9, and his ready acceptance of women as prophets and leaders in church life certainly demonstrates that he refused to be bound by culture or religious heritage when the gospel and its proclamation were at stake.[137]

Specific Instructions for Specific Situations

One contentious issue in some sections of the church today is the use to which specific scriptural directions and instructions may be used in establishing and maintaining a doctrine and practice for contemporary congregations. The more specific a piece of apostolic rule or direction for the writer's audience, the more important that we seek to understand fully both what he is writing and why he wrote what he did. This responsibility grows in intensity when a church attempts to apply some specific rule from a 'then and there' situation to a contemporary setting, very different from the original audience.

Some of the difficulty facing the theologian can be illustrated from my personal experience in relation to sermon preparation. On file in two church archives are some 1200 sermon manuscripts, each of them, (except for the first half dozen written in student days without any particular congregation in mind), prepared with specific congregations or groups in mind. While some of these sermons could be used in a context different from that for which they were originally intended, (and have on occasion been revised and preached to other congregations), the more specific the situation the sermon was addressing, the less useful it would be for any another audience. With the passage of time, the particular circumstances, which prompted certain of the applications made in the sermon, are not always immediately apparent even to me. At the time, it was prepared and preached, the sermon (I hope) was clear and relevant to the situation; but its value for another congregation at another time, with different needs and problems would be very, very limited.

Speaking more generally, when a sermon is prepared and preached, there is no doubt in the preacher's mind that this is God's word for these people. The same sermon could not be preached 20 years later, to a different congregation, with different needs, with the same level of confidence. It would need to be extensively revised, even re-written. Where such a sermon proclaimed the message of God's acceptance of us sinners for Christ's sake, its value for today would be immediate, but if the preacher was dealing with some local pastoral problem closely related to the cultural, moral and religious setting of the period, such specificity would not be immediately applicable to the present day congregation.

When one cannot be certain what the problem or issue was that the writer of Scripture was addressing in his letter to a congregation, it would be rash to make some universal rule out of such a specific application of Scripture. Let's suppose that there was a major mix-up in the first century mail delivery service and letters of Paul were held up in the post for several decades, and then delivered to the wrong congregations, with addresses changed. Corinth gets the letter to the Philippians; the congregations in

Galatia get 1 Corinthians, the people in Philippi received the letter intended for the Galatians, and Titus gets the letter to Philemon. While each congregation or individual would find much of common and immediate value for them from the 'wrong' letters, there would also be a good deal of uncertainty and confusion arising out of specific directions and instructions. Once the mix up had been sorted out, and the historical situation for all the recipients clarified as to why the writer had made the comments that he did, then they would have discovered some applications also for them from the specific directions of the mis-delivered letters.

In the passages that have been reviewed, two specific directions frequently applied in the present day are: 'Women should be silent in the churches; they are not permitted to speak' (1 Corinthians 14:34); and 'I permit no woman to teach' (1 Timothy 2:12).There is sufficient evidence in the Corinthian correspondence to understand the reason for the specific direction to the wives in that congregation; on the other hand, the situation in Timothy's congregations calling for the instruction of 1 Timothy 2:11-12 is far less certain. One can construct a picture, but it is not at all in sharp focus.

In both passages, there are explanations in the texts themselves, which are most helpful in understanding the reasons for the specific directions. The nature of the speaking in 1 Corinthians 14:34 is explained by the next verse: 'Let them ask their husbands at home'. The teaching forbidden to women/wives in 1 Timothy 2:12 was of that kind where *authentein* was involved. In both instances, the 'then and there' situations, which confronted the reader almost two thousand years ago, are totally different from the 'here and now' of congregational worship in Australia in the twenty-first century. An integral part of the 'then and there' situation is the argumentation the writer of Scripture used, to support his regulations that women should be silent and that women should not teach. For wives in 1 Corinthians and 1 Timothy to speak, or teach, there would have been (apart from anything else), a disregarding of the wife's subordination to her husband.

If this then is the principle which provides a basis for the specific directions, we need to go further and inquire as to the validity of this arrangement for all time. Is subordination of wives to husbands some eternal truth? Part of the so-called 'orders of creation'? Is the principle so comprehensive that all women are to be in subjection to men? Or is it only wives who are to be subordinate to their husbands?

What I am seriously questioning is the validly of taking such specific directions, intended to meet particular congregational needs at the time, and applying such regulations to prevent women today from being called into the public ministry of the church. In the fairly recent past, these passages were also used to prevent women from serving as elders, and synodical delegates, voting at congregational meetings and serving as members of ruling boards in the church. But the LCA has progressively recognised that it could no longer justify excluding women from such leadership roles. The passages of Scripture it had used, it subsequently regarded as not having the sort of application to the here and now that it previously believed.

An even more recent development was the decision in 2018 by the Commission on Theology and Inter-Church Relations of the LCA to issue Theological Statements, which clearly rejected the previous applications of the self-same biblical texts to prevent women from being ordained into the ministry of the church.[138] Many would have seen that development as a modern-day example of how the Spirit guided the LCA to appreciate meanings and applications of Scripture differently from how it was understood sixty years earlier. (The majority of delegates at the most recent synodical convention agreed with this judgment, but not the two-thirds majority needed to approve this major change in theological perception.)

Context and Culture are of Paramount Consideration

Are the passages where the writer used the subordination of wives to their husbands as a principle of importance in his argument in 1 Corinthians 14:34-35 and 1 Timothy 2:11-12 a truth for all time, which the church must teach and confess, as some insist on? Is there any compelling reason why one should not regard such a belief as much part of the writer's personality, his frame of reference, as his beliefs about slaves, celibacy, the state, or the value of wine for stomach ills? Subordination of wives to husbands was as much warp and woof of Paul's religious heritage and his cultural background as freedom, justice, gender equality and a 'fair go for all' are part of ours.

Paul and others wrote what they did to people who were in a dynamic relationship with their culture. In seeking to bring God's saving plans and purposes to the people of their time and place, the writers utilise what they can of the cultural norms and values of their environment. In the instances where the biblical writers made use of subordination, they were concerned about good order, decency and appropriate conduct. They were determined that the Christian way should not be condemned by the world for overthrowing the established order and the recognised structures of the time. Is not the church, then, in our time, in carrying out its God-given mission to communities where equality is a way of life, negatively impacting on the church's image, by refusing to grant women equality with men, and accordingly placing an unnecessary obstacle in the way of the church's proclamation of the gospel?

Cultures change, and such changes have a considerable bearing on what both the church and society generally consider as fitting and proper. Gender equality has for decades been legislated and made a way of life in our country and many others, and most churches have come to accept this as a reality for their own teaching and practice – with a few notable exceptions! No one would be so foolish as to claim that because the LCA now permits women to become elders or delegates to synodical conventions that it has lost sight of some biblical teaching on account of pressure from the secular world. Rather, it has recognised that its previous teaching in this matter was not soundly based on the clear word of Scripture. Undoubtedly, the humane and fair practice of the world provided an added incentive to question what it had previously held and to support the world's attitude by its own practices.

Churches do change their teachings and practices. In my lifetime, Lutheran Churches in Australia (perhaps in Germany and the United States as well) gave direction to its members against dancing, life insurance, interest charging and similar social/moral questions of the time. There is no way in our time that such proposals would even be submitted for consideration at state or national conventions. The responses of the church to its culture do change. Paul himself demonstrated the far-reaching changes the gospel made in male-female relationships (Galatians 3:26-29; Ephesians 5:21-33;

1 Corinthians 11:2-16). There were clearly situations where in spite of the cultural norm that women were to be subordinate to their husbands, women were involved as leaders in public worship. This change was not a threat to the church's mission in the world, in fact it strengthened it.[139]

In Summary

The practice of making normative for 21st century churches specific directions that were addressed to specified problems in first and second century congregations, with different needs and with different cultural settings, implies that 'then and there' and 'here and now' are all one. In other words, that would mean that there has been no change, no history, no development of ideas, no change to women's role and status, no impact on society through 2000 years of gospel proclamation. Herman Pech has correctly pointed out that our God takes all of history seriously, and that most certainly includes the history of humankind since the first century. God uses:

> ... the course of history to let us recognise more clearly the implications of his saving will, as revealed in Christ, for the ongoing life of the church and of society. Social issues give God the opportunity to reveal more fully the ramification of the reconciliation which he had accomplished through Christ, as the church grows up and matures. God does not merely keep up with social change in the course of history; we believe he also directs it.[140]

We live at a time when women in most parts of the world enjoy emancipation such as they had not known in previous history. Though some sections of society do not always enthusiastically promote the principle, our society does accord women the right to fulfil whatever role they choose in life. When it is remembered that for much of the past 2000 years, the church has led society to positive reappraisals of human worth and dignity, and has instigated change to all manner of social conditions, which were dehumanising and oppressive, it is not only surprising, but extremely disturbing, that sections of the church have persisted in resisting the movement towards sexual equality. Those who persist in this attitude would argue that they have done so and continue to do so because of their obedience to the Word of God. But is subordination of wives to husbands in obedience to God's Word to us today?

Has not God also said something of great importance to the church through the improved status of women in our society? Do we not also have the Spirit of Truth to lead us to the truth, so that we can act in a God-pleasing way without having to replicate the social norms and values of 2000 years ago? Quite correctly, the church rejoices that the evil of slavery is rightly condemned and is being progressively eliminated. Ought not the church to rejoice also in the fact that God has been active through enlightened men and women and has secured for women a status unknown for the most part in apostolic times, and join with the rest of society in according them equal honour and shared responsibility with men in the church's ministry?

Dear reader, please maintain with me that in no way could this be considered harmful to the chief doctrine of our faith, nor that it is a repudiation of the authority of the Scriptures. Quite the contrary, it would be in full accord with the splendid vision proclaimed in Galatians 3:27 'In Christ there is neither male nor female, for you are all one in him'.

Chapter 7
Quo Vadis, LCA?

SEVENTY YEARS AGO, WHEN THE LECTURERS from Concordia and Immanuel Colleges and other church leaders met to consider possible ways to unite the Evangelical Lutheran Church of Australia (ELCA) and the United Evangelical Lutheran Church of Australia (UELCA), one of the many issues they needed to clarify and agree on was the church's ministry. The Second World War had finally ended. Millions had been killed. Millions who survived were refugees, seeking a new home in Australia, North and South America and in devastated parts of Europe and Asia.

In some parts of the world, the male population had been decimated more than the female. Women throughout the world had been involved in the war effort, not just on the home-front, but in occupations, duties and callings, previously restricted to men. With the war over, there was an on-going movement of women to combine teaching, nursing, secretarial duties and home responsibilities with professions formerly restricted to males. It seemed a natural progression, then, for women to be called and ordained into the office of the ministry – which previously had been exclusively male. Parts of Europe, particularly Denmark, Slovakia, Germany,

Norway and Sweden led the way in calling women into the office of the ministry in Lutheran and other churches.

Close Ties with Overseas Churches

The ELCA had, since the 1880s, strong ties with a branch of Lutheranism in the USA, the Lutheran Church - Missouri Synod (LCMS), one of the larger and probably the most conservative of Lutheran bodies in the United States, with a membership of two million. For a period of eight decades, a steady stream of ELCA theological lecturers and parish pastors had trained or undertaken post-graduate studies in Missouri Synod seminaries at Fort Wayne and St Louis. LCMS dignitaries and theologians regularly visited 'down under'. The Lutheran Hour, produced by the LCMS, with American speakers, was for decades proudly sponsored and widely promoted by the ELCA. Sunday school materials, devotional books, theological journals (e.g. CTM), and other literature were eagerly read and endorsed by ELCA pastors and parishioners. LCMS text books were used for many years at Concordia Seminary, Adelaide (ELCA). Australian church leaders were regularly the recipients of honorary Doctor of Divinity degrees from Concordia Seminary, St Louis. The LCMS was known to be one of the most ultra-conservative branches of Lutheranism, insisting for example, on the inerrancy of Scripture and the need to avoid unionism (not the trade union variety, but rather not having altar and pulpit fellowship with churches that were not as confessional as they were).

The UELCA was conservative in theology like the ELCA; but it had closer historical links with branches of German Lutheran Churches rather than with American Lutheran Churches. Some of its theologians and parish pastors had trained or undertaken post-graduate studies in German universities and theological seminaries. It had membership in the Lutheran World Federation (LWF), an association that the ELCA had strongly rejected, because it regarded some member churches of the LWF as not being theologically conservative enough.

During negotiations to unite the two Lutheran Churches in Australia, the UELCA's membership in the LWF was a continuing obstacle until finally the UELCA agreed to end its membership in the international organisation. The UELCA and the ELCA traced their origins to the disagreements between the two initial German immigrant pastors, Kavel and Fritzsche, and their South Australia congregations in the 1840-50s. For decades, Lutheran pastors and their congregations in South Australia, Victoria and Queensland formed and reformed groups of synods (at one stage there were five!), until in 1926 the UELCA was finally established and then the ELCA in 1944 after undertaking its final name change.

The Decision to Exclude Women

It was quite remarkable that theologians and parish pastors from both Lutheran Churches in Australia, after more than a century of separate and not always friendly co-existence, with serious differences, could, after the end of the Second World War, sit down together, pray together and try to resolve previous misunderstandings, and agree on teachings and practices that were previously used as reasons to keep the two churches apart. Theses on the church's ministry, prepared initially by Dr F. Blaess (ELCA) and Dr Hebart (UELCA), and endorsed by joint committees in May 1950, after describing in detail the historic Lutheran understanding of the church's ministry on the basis of Scripture and the Lutheran Confessions, concluded the theses with a statement that excluded women from the church's ministry:

> 1 Cor. 14:34-35 and 1 Tim. 2:8-15 prohibit a woman from being called into the office of the public ministry for the proclamation of the Word and the administration of the Sacraments. This apostolic rule is binding on all Christendom; hereby her rights as a member of the spiritual priesthood are in no wise impaired.

These verses from the New Testament were used, both before and after the LCA was established in 1966, to prevent women from holding voting membership in congregations, from being elected as elders or major office holders in congregations, from representing their congregations at state and national conventions, and from becoming a member of policy-making boards of the national Church. These legalistic prohibitions have progressively been removed, but not the prohibition excluding women from the office of the ministry.

One might try to understand why the lecturers from both seminaries and other church leaders in the 1950s should have made the decision to exclude women from the church's ministry. It was a matter for serious discussion in some European churches. There can be little doubt that the close relationship of LCMS was a strong influence in the decision-making process. There were probably other influences. An obvious reason for the decree against women in ministry can be found, of course, in their understanding of the texts they quoted. We may rightly assume that they came to this understanding of the texts because, on the surface, they seemed to support such conclusions, and such conclusions would be in accord with the male-dominating culture of the Lutheran Churches in Australia. They probably found support for their views from European theologians. Only later did some doubts arise and one of the lecturers attempted (unsuccessfully) to prove that both texts were trying to teach the same.[141]

But we need to go further and take into account the culture prevailing in the Lutheran Churches in Australia in the 1950s, where the thought of male-female equality was years away in the predominantly rural communities where the churches were strongly represented. As a visiting student preacher in many congregations in Queensland and South Australia during the 50s, not once did I hear a hint of protest or even of mild disagreement, with what the Inter-synodical Committees had written. It is possible that the Theses on Ministry were not widely publicised. The people responsible for the exclusion of women from the ministry were not challenged to support their claim, certainly not by the women of the church who had traditionally accepted whatever the male clergy told them; for the male clergy, apart from those who read German, Danish or Norwegian church magazines, the issue of female pastors was probably too remote, and therefore not a matter for debate.

The fact that some European churches were introducing female clergy was probably due to a shortage of male pastors, they might well have reasoned. What the leaders of both churches had decided was probably a safe-guard against such an intrusion into the church happening in this part of the world. It's not our problem here! We have ample male candidates! So, it is not an issue! Be it said, to my shame, that I, and, as far as I can recall, none of my fellow seminarians raised any questions when the theological lecturers told us of the exclusion of women from the ministry. The fact that LCMS had not accepted female pastors would probably have given additional weight to the faculty's decision.[142] (Subsequently, at least three of my contemporaries in training joined the LCMS, a further indication of the strong fraternal and theological ties ELCA had with the LCMS.)

Changes in Teaching and Practice

The ABC program *Four Corners* that went to air on 19 May 2020 clearly demonstrated the divisions between and among political parties concerning climate change and what action should be taken to reduce carbon pollution. As I watched the sad story unfold, of elections won and lost, of prime ministers removed and replaced, of debates continued, and the way forward in dealing with the crisis confused, confusing and unresolved, I shared some of the sadness and anger that high-ranking public servants and scientists expressed, because the challenge had not been unitedly addressed. Perhaps others who are aware of the divisions and distress experienced within the LCA over the issue of women's ordination may have seen some parallels between the political scene and what has been taking place in the LCA through much of its short history.

Some important changes have been made: women can now be elected to leadership positions in their congregations, to represent their congregations at state and national conventions, to policy- and decision-making boards and councils of the LCA. But the ordination of women into the ministry of the LCA failed to secure the two-thirds majority at the last national Synod, a requirement for this important change to become a reality.

Churches Benefit from Women in Public Ministry

Surely no one can seriously and honestly claim that the outreach, pastoral care and teaching responsibilities of local congregations have now been weakened in any way because of the involvement of women as elders, chairpersons and lay-readers in LCA congregations! The fact that women are now represented at synodical meetings of the LCA has not led the church to take actions and make decisions that have been harmful to Christ's mission in our land (apart from not agreeing to women's ordination!). I have no first-hand knowledge of the consequences of having women sharing fully with men in decision-making, planning, and leading in all aspects of congregational and synodical life in the LCA, but I am thoroughly and thankfully aware of the many positive benefits of women's sharing leadership, teaching and administrative roles with men in the witness, fellowship and outreach of congregations, presbyteries and synods in the Uniting Church.

The first time Cynthia and I attended a Lutheran service in the United States in 1978, I was initially surprised that a woman was the preacher and the celebrant, but five minutes into the service, the gender of the preacher was totally irrelevant, as she proclaimed the good news with authority and appeal. The minister was not a pastor of the LCMS, but of the Evangelical Lutheran Church of America (ELCA), whose seminary I was about to attend in St Paul, Minnesota, on a scholarship from the same church. The advantages of having female ministers soon became apparent in the more progressive ELCA. Their presence in the pulpit and as the celebrants at the Lord's Table was an obvious and compelling repudiation of sexual discrimination in that church. Even in the conservative mid-west of the USA, women were gladly accepted and treasured as the messengers of Christ and were quickly able to bring their special gifts and qualities in the service of Christ to congregations, hospitals, theological institutions and highly demanding leadership positions in the regional and national church. The current President of the largest Lutheran Seminary in the United States (Luther Seminary, St Paul, Minn.) is a woman, the Rev. Dr Robin Steinke. The Presiding Bishop of the three million strong ELCA, the Reverend Elizabeth Eaton, has recently been re-elected for a further five-year term. In 2020, the ELCA will celebrate with real thanksgiving the 50th anniversary of the ordination of women into the ministry of the Lutheran Church in the USA.

Why Does the LCA Persist in Excluding Women?

In all honesty I must ask, why the hesitation, no, the determined resistance, on the part of a diminishing number of LCA clergy and lay-persons of having women in the ministry of the Australian Lutheran Church? Is it a fear of women and what may become of the LCA with women in positions of leadership? Are some male clergy threatened by females' seeming 'intrusion' into a previously male exclusive domain? Do opponents of female pastors fear that with women in the pastoral office, the theology so precious will be undermined and the Good News will no longer be heard?

I have worked and worshipped for 40 years in congregations of the Uniting Church, where women as well as men are ministers, chaplains, moderators, (equivalent to bishops),

General Secretaries (an office of leadership and authority), and national Presidents and where the gender of the person has been of no consequence. When congregations are searching for a replacement minister, no one bothers to ask about the gender of possible candidates. When the Uniting Church was formed with the coming together of Methodist, Presbyterian and Congregational Churches, ministers in good standing from those churches, male and female, were readily accepted as ministers in the new church. At the present time, at least half of the ministers in the Uniting Church in Tasmania and Victoria are females. The special qualities and characteristics that females can bring to the office of ministry are gifts that enrich interpersonal relationships and pastoral ministry. As women, they can often provide new insights into the meaning and application of biblical texts.

Given the experience of many churches (including the majority of Lutheran Churches throughout the world) where women share the ministry of Word and sacraments with men, why then the determined reluctance on the part of some pastors and lay persons in the LCA to invite and encourage suitably qualified and trained female persons from entering the church's ordained ministry? Is it due to a refusal to accept male-female equality in the LCA, as though such acceptance might be a rejection of some biblical principle? Is it because their interpretation of two biblical texts (i.e. that women are excluded from the office of the ministry) is regarded as the only possible application these texts must have for the 21st century churches? Is it because, if they now authorise the ordination of female persons, they are rejecting what Lutheran leaders in this country seventy years ago maintained, and that is something they are unwilling to do? Is the tradition of always having male ministers in Australian

Lutheran Churches the deciding factor? Is it because Christ chose 12 males to be his apostles, and thus only males can be ministers of Word and sacraments?

Theses of Agreement

Must the final paragraph of the Theses of Agreement be regarded as an immutable decree that must be retained, no matter how questionable the exegesis used to support it? No doubt those who drafted and endorsed the Theses on Ministry, which pronounced that women cannot have part in this work, believed the oft-quoted texts clearly determined the answer for their time. But must the church, seventy years later, continue to endorse their thinking? As was shown in the earlier exegesis of these passages, to claim that these texts prohibit the church in the 21st century from ordaining women into the office of the ministry is a misuse of what these passages are saying to us; they are dealing with altogether different situations.[143]

The fact that women were engaged in the work of ministry in first century congregations with the full support of Paul and others would mean that their activity would later stand condemned, prohibited by 1 Corinthians 14:34-35 and 1 Timothy 2:8-15, if these texts were intended to exclude women from this work in our time. If they were written to exclude women in our time from the ministry, then they would have to have been passing judgment also on the apostles and congregations who had thankfully accepted the ministry of these women!

Thus the question that men and women of the LCA are being forced to debate, year after year, from one synodical convention to the next, is, do we, or don't we, continue to prevent women, because of their gender, from serving their Lord, as men have been doing since the LCA was established, as ministers of the church? Shall we continue to exclude them from serving in the office of the public ministry just because they are women, and for that reason disqualified from serving with their gifts in a calling where the gospel of Jesus Christ is publicly proclaimed and the sacraments administered in an orderly and responsible manner?

Shall we continue to disown and reject society's insistence of gender equality and instead maintain the myth of thousands of years ago that women must be subordinate to men? Shall we insist on maintaining this mistaken notion by claiming that the Scriptures demand this of us? Shall we claim that the Theses of Agreement, which are part of the LCA's history, expect this of us for all time? That we cannot amend and correct their theses, even though the document gives the church the authority to do so?

Constitution, By-laws and Synodical Procedures

The LCA Constitution, in *Article 5. The Ministry*, speaks in 5.1 'of men whose qualifications for the office of the ministry...' It would appear that it would be necessary to amend the sentence to include women as well as men, if the existing wording is advanced as a reason for the exclusion of women from this office.

The By-Laws of the LCA's Constitution (7.3.28.2) require that 'a matter deemed to be of a theological or confessional nature which has been referred to the General Pastors' Conference (GFC) for consideration shall be considered by the convention only after a recommendation has been received from the General Pastors' Conference.' The By-Laws also state (7.3.28.3)

'For a resolution on a matter of doctrine to be deemed to be the official position of the Church, it shall require a two-thirds majority of all registered delegates at the convention'.

The 2015 General Convention of the LCA asked the CTICR to build on its earlier work regarding the ordination of women and men to develop a draft doctrinal statement for General Pastors' Conference (GPC) and the 19th Convention of the Synod that presents:

- a theological basis for the ordination of women and men; and
- a theological basis for why the ordination of women and men need not be church divisive.[144]

The Draft Doctrinal statement prepared by CTICR called 'A Theological Basis for the Ordination of Women and Men' was discussed at some length by the GPC and then the pastors voted on the following statement 'Do you support changing the Church's teaching to that contained in the Draft Doctrinal Statement on the Ordination of Women and Men?' The result was Yes 44.5%, No 55%., with one ballot blank.[145]

The 2018 General Convention of Synod debated this issue over three sessions. Finally, a vote was taken on the following resolution:

1. That the Lutheran Church of Australia amend its public teaching to accept the ordination of both women and men;
2. That Synod affirms the church's teaching on the ministry contained in paragraphs one to ten of Theses of Agreement VI: Theses on the Office of the Ministry;

3. That Synod adopts 'A theological basis for the ordination of women and men' as the teaching of the church, replacing the teaching contained in TA VI.11;
4. The LCA/NZ invite properly gifted, trained, prepared and called women to serve as ordained pastors alongside of male pastors of this church, exercising the office of the keys by proclaiming the Gospel, pronouncing absolution, and administering the sacraments, to the glory of God and for the extension of his Kingdom;
5. That Synod directs the General Church Council to attend to the necessary administrative arrangements required to facilitate the entry of women into the office of the public ministry.

Bishop Henderson subsequently declared to the Synod that, by a secret ballot, the motion was lost with 240 votes in favour and 159 against, with 2 informal and 5 abstentions. The motion was lost as the required two thirds majority of 271 was not reached. The chair thanked everyone for the good order with which they conducted themselves during the debate. After the result was announced, during the Saturday morning, a session of Convention was dedicated to allow time for the delegates to discuss in small table groups how they were feeling and to give voice to their hopes and fears. The District Bishops circulated around the tables to listen to conversations and reported back on what they had heard. A resolution was subsequently adopted 'That Synod acknowledge the deep hurt in the course of the debate on ordination and seeks reconciliation'.[146]

Bishop Henderson reported a month later 'We know that, while we are holding together, we are nevertheless a divided church. That is our reality. Bishop David Altus reflectively summarised what he heard during the table conversations during Convention as the LCA/NZ is "hurting".[147]

What the LCA Continues to Teach and Practise

By a handful of votes, the LCA/NZ has persisted in its refusal to ordain women, though a strong majority of delegates clearly favoured such a change. But the decision has been made and the Church remains divided. Since the requirement of the By-Laws has not been met, it is the whole church, not just the small minority that has to take responsibility for the decision. By treating women as unfit for the ministry, is not the LCA sadly declaring that suitably qualified, trained, gifted and dedicated women are not intelligent, strong, competent, or committed enough to qualify for this office of service in the church as preachers, teachers, counsellors, administrators because of their gender? That is the impression that continues to be conveyed. Thus, the church is in danger of continuing to create serious offence (cf. Matthew 18:6). A pastor of the LCA after meeting with male and female ministers from every continent (except Australia) wrote in respect to the offence caused by the exclusion of women from the church's ministry:

> ... one cannot maintain that women and girls are co-equally created in God's image and are co-equally children of God when they are, at the same time, being dehumanised and oppressed due to their gender. If women and girls are (*in effect*) taught (*by the ordering of ministry in the church*) that their creation in God's image has the divine imprint to a lesser degree, we can only expect the Holy Spirit to assure them that they are loved

by God (*who is love, and in whose image they were created*) in spite of the ordering of the ministry in the church, not as result of it.[148]

Another pastor of the LCA – one of the thirty who read and responded to my DOCTOR OF MINISTRY thesis forty years ago – included this telling observation in his reaction to what I had written:

> The thing that saddens me is that instead of the church being at the forefront of the movement for a new definition of the roles and relationships of women, we are at the rear – more than this, we are acting as a sheet anchor against the new freedoms and humanising of relationships. A change is inevitable. We will have women ministers in the LCA by the turn of the century, but I am sad for the pain which will come to many on the way. We have a church mentality which is so legalistic in spite of our evangelical professions and protestations... the trouble is that it so hard to change an old and rather rigid structure without the thing falling on top of some people who are finding it to be a very safe and secure refuge.[149]

His prediction, and undoubted hope, of having women ministers in the LCA by the turn of the century was not realised, but the other prediction – the sad one – of the pain that some would experience is clearly a reality. It was widely reported that when the proposal to ordain both women and men was not passed by the necessary two thirds majority, there was profound sorrow and deep disappointment over the result.

A resolution agreed to at the last synodical conference 'A Theological Basis for why the Ordination of Women and Men Need Not be Church Divisive', declared *inter alia*:

3. ... the ongoing disagreement about the interpretation of and application of the two texts that have been at the centre of the LCA debate (1 Cor. 14:33b-36; 1 Tim. 2:11-15) is a matter of exegetical opinion, and does not affect ...key church teaching, and is therefore not church divisive.
4. The Lutheran doctrine of the ministry, clearly spelt out in the Augsburg Confession 5 and 14, contains nothing that excludes women from entering the ranks of the ministry...
5. The Theses of Agreement themselves make it clear that, as new issues and new questions arise, the Church has the liberty to examine its teaching afresh in the light of the Scripture and the Confessions, 'and accordingly confirm them, or amend them, or repudiate them when further study of God's Word shows them to be inadequate or in error'.
6. If the Church were to ordain women and men, some in the Church may remain conscience-bound to the teaching that ordination is for men only. This would have implications for church polity and for people's reception of the means of grace within the worship life of the Church. These matters are at the very heart of the life of the Church. The Church has the responsibility to engage in the ongoing task of addressing this in such a way that the ministry of the gospel is not hindered, Christian love is upheld, and every effort is made to 'maintain the unity of the Spirit in the bond of peace' (Eph. 4:3).[150]

Post 2018 Convention

A month after the 2018 Sydney Convention of the LCA had failed to endorse the proposal of the church's CTICR to ordain women, the presiding Bishop of the LCA, the Reverend John Henderson, wrote *inter alia*:

> Some of us were relieved at the decision but can still empathise with those who feel differently. Others express impatience with any talk of empathy or pain; after four votes they don't want any further discussion.
>
> Some of us who hold passionately to a male-only pastorate now believe that the LCA needs to learn how to think rightly. They are tempted to include things the LCA does not teach, such as male headship and subordination based on orders of creation. Some of us have personal views on these matters, but pastors and teachers must not burden consciences by giving the impression that our church teaches them. What we do teach is that in Christ there is a new creation (2 Corinthians 5:17) in which all are equal in him (Galatians 3:28).
>
> After the vote at Convention some of us, deeply saddened and struggling with the decision, immediately resigned from all responsibilities in the church, and a few, heartbreakingly, from the LCA/NZ itself. Others may feel like doing so, but are holding back out of concern for partners, families, congregations and the people in ministries in which they serve. Some people

who initially felt pain and anger at the decision have moved on to a reluctant acceptance....

And, of course, many of you faithful, committed Christians aren't involved in these disturbances. For your sake I have hesitated to write about these things. You show us that, no matter what, God's work goes on. The church continues in its baptismal grace, practising mutual forgiveness, demonstrating the love of Christ, feeding the hungry and clothing the naked, and committing those who have died to the eternal care of their Lord. Let's not lose sight of that. It is why God had put us here, for the sake of the gospel.

I don't believe the ordination of women is, of itself, our main issue. It's a 'presenting issue' that springs from somewhere deeper down. We must now explore what that is. For decades we have prepared carefully formulated theological statements and tried not to rock the boat by moving too far to one side or the other. Now there is a sense that we need something more, something to tell us clearly who we are and how we will work together for the Kingdom even though there are, and it seems will remain, things on which we cannot agree.

This situation is a serious challenge to the LCA/NZ's usual methodology of argument and counter-argument, conferences and conventions, constitutions and votes. Twenty-plus years of doing those things has not brought us together on this issue. Along the way, of course, we have learned some good things, such as mutual respect, calling out bad behaviour, and acknowledging that both sides of the debate take Scripture and Confessions seriously. We have also learned many new things from Scripture. Since this Convention, however, members want more. They are asking their leaders and each other for a new way of resolving our difference, a third way, one that holds Christ at the centre of our faith, honours all participants, and keeps the LCA/NZ together.

So there is work to do. To do it well we need to do it together....[151]

On 27 February 2019, Bishop Henderson reported on a meeting of the College of Bishops and the General Church Board *inter alia*:

> We face critical issues: determining the will of God in his Word on certain issues; impatience with Synod's processes which do not seem to be solving differences; intemperance in some quarters towards others who do not agree with them on certain points; and for some an understanding but for others a distressing testing of the limits or 'boundaries' by which we regulate the church's faith and life...
>
> The LCA, as a community of faith, is at a spiritual turning point. God is teaching us, yet again, to wait patiently for him, trust him and put all our burdens on him. It is a time of temptation, wanting to find our own way and forgetting to wait for God. It is a time when the human spirit, out of understandable frustration, wants to 'fix' things and put them back on track. It is a time for

us to cry out to God, not only for guidance, but also for enough faith to trust him with everything we have, up to and including the church.

I am certain that God has given us more than enough resources to meet these challenges head on.[152]

On March 2020, Bishop Henderson reported on another meeting of the College of Bishops and the General Church Board *inter alia*:

> The reason for the meeting was to consider what has been happening in our church since the 2018 General Convention of Synod …We remain deeply divided on the issue, and continue to experience unrest. As a result, some congregations and individuals are taking bold actions of one kind or another. People are asking, 'What happens next, given that we don't agree with each other?'
>
> LCA leaders are not adopting a 'knee jerk' respond to this disquiet. They want to listen and understand, include and not exclude. While we know that this can frustrate those who want a quicker solution, we must take a 'long view', wanting to preserve the truth, unity and witness of the church. District bishops and councils are in dialogue with congregations and pastors as they need to be…
>
> I strongly urge all of you who feel disaffected by our current circumstances to consider deeply and prayerfully the type and nature of any actions you may be planning to undertake in response. I know this demands much from us, perhaps more

than we feel we can give. We are disturbed by issues of faithfulness and truth, justice and equity. Feelings can be high, spurred on by anxiety for our future, and that of the church. Such anxiety clouds our judgment. We should not let that cause us to speak ill of others, or harm them in any way.

I pray that through God's love we will receive the grace we need to work through our differences. He is trustworthy and true. For surely, we all agree on what is most important, that God's forgiving love brings light and life to all people. We are here to praise God and bring that message to a dying and darkening world.[153]

So, *Quo Vadis*, LCA/NZ?

Lutherans in Australia and New Zealand, caught up in the unresolved disagreement over the question whether women, and not just men, ought to be called into the office of the ministry, have been fortunate to have such a calming, evangelical leader as Bishop John Henderson. He, along with his predecessors, and parish pastors, theological lecturers, and thousands of men and women in congregations throughout the Church have worked, prayed, debated and negotiated with untiring patience to resolve the division so that LCA/NZ might unitedly and without distractions devote itself once again to the far weightier tasks the church has been commissioned to undertake.

As long as it remains a contentious issue with women excluded from the opportunity of using their gifts and dedication in the office of the church's ministry, the LCA/NZ is not only depriving its membership of their service, it is also saying in effect that females are disqualified from serving in this way for no other reason than that they are females. The sad reality is that in persisting with this teaching the Church is continuing to cause offence, alienating women and men, males and females, who share equally in the new order of oneness through being baptised in Christ.

For my part, I have been spared most of the anguish and frustration many of my former colleagues and parishioners have endured during the past 40 years. When I resigned from the Lutheran Church's ministry it was not because I could foresee the anguish ahead, it was rather because the leave of absence I sought to undertake a ministry for five years as Director of Pastoral Care and Community Education in a non-Lutheran church, was refused. I have had no regrets for taking the action I did. Without being caught up in the never-ending debates over what offices and roles women could engage in the LCA/NZ, I was able to utilise and develop gifts in ministry for previously unimagined outreach and service.

In addition to, and as an extension of my regular preaching, teaching, pastoral care and counselling, courses and groups were organised for couples to enrich and strengthen their life together, for persons caring for relatives with dementia and other long term illnesses, for parents raising children with major disabilities, for persons enduring ongoing grief following a bereavement or other major loss, for couples planning to marry or remarry (with children from a former relationship), for ministers and celebrants intent on assisting couples as they planned their marriage and their life together, for people wanting to know what the Christian religion is all about prior to joining a Christian church, for psychologists and social workers supporting caregivers of persons with dementia, for ministers and lay leaders intent on providing a stronger ministry to the older members in their congregations.

In all these activities, my wife, Cynthia, was directly involved. Individually and together, we published ten books and training manuals, with Cynthia a frequent writer for peer-reviewed journals.[154] These courses, groups and publications grew out of our work environment – Cynthia as founder and editor of the *Journal of Family Studies* and senior lecturer in the Faculty of Health Sciences at La Trobe University and me as a minister in two Melbourne Churches and, after retirement, as relieving minister in eight Melbourne congregations and as the Synod Coordinator of Ministry to Older Persons in Victoria and Tasmania.

While Cynthia and I were engaged in our demanding and often innovative work, we observed, from a distance, the progress and the delays as the LCA/NZ sought to arrive at a consensus on male-female equality. As we read and re-read Bishop John's sad analysis of the division, unrest and uncertainty prevailing in the Church, we grieve with the many who feel ongoing loss for what has not yet been achieved, we want to encourage Bishop John and all Bishops and leaders in the Church to persevere in their endeavours. For our part, there has been no doubt since writing my DMin thesis forty years ago that gender equality needs to be expressed in all areas of the Church's life. We feel relief that in most areas that were formerly male-exclusive, the LCA/NZ now encourages women to participate, using their gifts and experiences to enrich the lives and deepen the work of congregations and the church at large.

In answer to the question posed at the beginning of this chapter 'Quo vadis, LCA?', it is our earnest prayer that it is not heading into sectarian division, fragmentation and a repudiation of the unity of faith and practice it confidently displayed in 1966, when in good faith and with determination to work and worship together, it was founded. We are certainly aware that Lutheranism in Australia has, at different periods in its history, displayed a tendency to disunity and fragmentation and not always for sound theological reasons. Having been a deaconess before our marriage, Cynthia also had personal knowledge of this history.

We earnestly hope that the LCA/NZ will soon, after years of debate, finally and unitedly decide to make it possible for women to train and be equipped for ministry and be welcomed with sincerity and thanksgiving into congregations as their called servants of Christ. We have no doubt that when that eventuates, the LCA/NZ will recognise how greatly it benefits from their ministries. We believe that by welcoming women into the Church's ministry, it will not be repudiating any doctrine of the faith, nor will it be disregarding any clear teaching of Scripture; instead, it will be acting in accordance with the great revolutionary declaration of Paul in Galatians 3:26-28: 'For in Christ Jesus you are all the children of God through faith. As many of you as were baptised into Christ have clothed yourself with Christ. There is no longer Jew nor Greek, there is no longer slave nor free, there is no longer male nor female, for all of you are one in Christ Jesus'.

End notes

[1] Matthew 20:24-28; Luke 22:24-27; John 13:1-16; Acts 11:29; Romans 13:11; 2 Corinthians 4:1; Ephesians 4:1-16; Philippians 1:1; Colossians 1:25; 1 Timothy 3:8-13.

[2] 1 Corinthians 3:5-4:5; 12:4-30; 2 Corinthians 3:4-4:6; 1 Peter 4:10.

[3] Ephesians 3:7; Mark 10:45; 2 Corinthians 5:11-6:10; 8:9; 9:12-15; Act 3.

[4] Hulme, *Two Ways of Caring* (Minneapolis: Augsburg Publishing House, 1973)

[5] A Morley, *A Gathering of Strangers* (Philadelphia: Westminster Press, 1976) 95.

[6] Morley, *A Gathering*, 109.

[7] Faculty of Christ Seminary, 'For the Ordination of Women,' *Currents in Theology and Mission* 6 (1979), 138.

[8] Clemens E Hoopmann, 'Woman's Place in the Congregation with special Reference to Woman Suffrage,' *Official Report of the Forty Third Convention of the Evangelical Lutheran Concordia Conference of New Zealand*, Upper Moutere, (May 1954) 6.

[9] Ibid., 7.

[10] 'VI: Theses on the Office of the Ministry' *Theses of Agreement*, 1950, Lutheran Church of Australia.

[11] CTICR concluded their report on 'The Role of Women in the Church' with the statement 'Since no clear case can be made out for the view that acting as delegates at democratically organised conventions is really an unbiblical exercise of authority, the right to act as delegates at conventions of the Church may be granted to men and women alike', *Book of Reports*, 1978 Synod: 288. Synod, however, resolved to defer a decision, requesting reports be submitted to Pastors' Conferences and congregations prior to next Synod Convention. *Minutes*, p. 52, 1978 Synod.

End notes

[12] 'Statement on the Rights of Women to Vote at Meetings of the Congregation' General Synod of the Lutheran Church of Australia, 1968.

[13] Ibid.

[14] In 2018 the Commission on Theology and Church Relations of the LCA released the following Principal Documents in preparation for the General Convention later that year: 'A theological basis for the ordination of women and men', and 'A theological basis for why the ordination of women and men need not be church divisive', and Supplementary Documents 'A theological basis for the ordination of women and men: background to the Draft Doctrinal Statement' and 'Engaging with the Draft Doctrinal Statement: reflections arising from the current teaching of the Lutheran Church'.

On receipt of these documents I forwarded a response to the presiding Bishop of the LCA (Rev. John Henderson) 'Bishop John, Let me express my congratulations to you and to the CTICR for the progressive, emphatic, daring and critically important Draft Doctrinal Statements and Commentaries. Since writing my DMin thesis in May 1981 I have often wished that LCA theologians would publicly acknowledge the need to review and correct the misuse made of 1 Corinthians 14:33b-36 and 1 Timothy 2:11-15 in the 'Theses of Agreement' and in other official documents of the LCA (and the previous ELCA). Now at long last there is a public acknowledgment that the two passages have been misunderstood and misapplied when used as the reason for refusing to permit women to share in the ministry of Word and sacrament... After all these years I still have not given up hope that the LCA would recognise the need to stop taking passages out of a very different cultural/religious context and misapply them to our very different world/church. Maybe that day is almost here'. Sadly, the General Convention in 2018 did not agree to the ordination of women.

[15] David W. Preus, 'From the President, Striving Towards Justice and Equity,' *The Lutheran Standard*, April 17, 1979, 36: 'The 1970 general convention of the American Lutheran Church (ALC) voted to ordain women. The 1972 convention adopted a statement, 'Women and Men in Church and Society'. The opening paragraph of the statement declares 'The American Lutheran Church is pleased to see that strides being made in church and society to recognise the rights of women. Such strides are matters of simple justice

and equity'. Those words are as appropriate today as they were then. We are making progress'.

[16] See Chapter 7.

[17] 'We believe, teach and confess that the sole rule and standard according to which all dogmas together with all teachers should be estimated and judged are the prophetic and apostolic Scriptures of the Old and New Testament alone.' Epitome of the Articles in Controversy, 1, *Triglotta*, 779.

[18] 1. Madeleine Boucher, 'Some Unexplored Explored Parallels to 1 Cor.11:11-12 and Gal. 3:28: The N.T. on the Role of Women,' *The Catholic Biblical Quarterly* 31 (1969) 50; G B Caird, 'Paul and Women's Liberty,' Bulletin of John Rylands Library 54 (Spring 1972) 271; Jo Duisman, 'Concluding Unscientific Postscript on Women in the Church,' *The Lutheran Witness*, March 1968, 77; Elizabeth Schüssler Fiorenza, 'Women in the Pre-Pauline and Pauline Churches,' *Union Seminary Quarterly* 33 (Spring and Summer 1978) 153; David and Eloise Fraser, 'A Biblical View of Women: Demythologizing Sexegesis,' *Theology, News and Notes*, June 1975, 17; Nancy Hardesty, 'The Status of Evangelical Women,' *The Reformed Journal* July-August 1973, 4; William E. Hull, 'Woman in Her Place: Biblical Perspectives,' *Review and Exposition* (Winter 1975) 8; Henry P. Hamann, 'The New Testament and the Ordination of Women,' *Lutheran Theological Journal* 9 (December 1975) 101; George W. Knight, 'The New Testament Teaching on the Role Relationship of Male and Female with Special Reference to the Teaching/Ruling Functions in the Church,' *Journal of Psychology and Theology* 3 (Summer 1975) 218; Lutheran Church of Australia, *Official Report of the Constituting Convention of the First General Synod* (Tanunda, S.A, 1966, 97; 'A Theological Basis for the Ordination of Women and Men', and 'A Theological Basis for the Ordination of Women and Men: Background to the Draft Doctrinal Statement', Prepared by the CTICR for the General Convention of Synod 2018; Thomas R W Longstaff, 'The Ordination of Women: A Biblical Perspective', *Anglican Theological Review* 57 (March 1975) 317; Wayne A Meeks, 'The Image of the Androgyne: Some Uses of a Symbol in the Earliest Christianity,' *History of Religions* 13 (February 1974) 166; Elaine Pagels, 'Paul and Women: A Response to Recent Discussions,' *Journal of the American Academy of Religion* 42 (September 1974) 539; Connie Parvey, 'Ordain Her, Ordain Her Not', *Dialog* 8 (Summer 1969), 203; Robin Scroggs 'Paul and the Eschatological Woman Revisited,' *Journal of the American Academy of Religion* 42 (1974) 553; Krister Stendahl 'Women in the Churches,' *Soundings* 53 (Winter 1970) 376; Sacred Congregation for

the Doctrine of the Faith, 'Declaration on the Question of the Admission of Women to the Ministerial Priesthood,' *Women Priests* eds. Leonard Swidler and Arlene Swidler (New York: Pauline Press, 1977), 42; Michael J Williams 'The Man/Woman Relationship in the New Testament,' *Churchman* 91 (January 1977) 35; Wm O Walker Jr. '1 Corinthians 11:2-16 and Paul's Views Regarding Women,' *Journal of Biblical Literature* 94 (March 1975) 94; Report on the Commission of Theology and Church Relations, the Lutheran Church-Missouri Synod, 'Woman Suffrage in the Church,' 4; Adela Yarbro Collins, 'No longer 'Male and Female' (Gal. 3:28),' *Journal of Ethics and Christianity*, 1 (2019) 27-39; Bruce Hansen *All of You are One*, 67-103.

[19] Karen Neutel, *A Cosmopolitan Ideal*, 239: 'Paul's eschatological perspective can also illuminate our understanding of his thought on the law. Seeing the importance of this perspective allows us to understand the radical nature of Paul's statement about the Jewish law...Paul assumes that God has taken a new step in sending Christ, thereby allowing both Jew and gentiles access to God on the same grounds of 'faith in Christ', that the law no longer functions as a characteristic of those who belong to Christ.'

[20] Meeks, 180ff; Scroggs, 291; H D Betz, 'Spirit, Law and Freedom: Paul's Message to the Galatian Churches', *Svensk Exeg. Arsbok* 39 (1974), 145-160; Adela Yarbro Collins 'No longer 'Male and Female' (Gal.3: 28),'*JEAC* 1 2019, 28.

[21] Tanya Wittwer, 'Subordination and Headship: A Case Study in Lutheran Hermeneutics',*LTJ* 53/1, (2019) 23 points out that 'The core of a Lutheran hermeneutics is that we read and interpret the Bible in the light of God's free gift of grace. This tradition leads us to begin a Biblical overview of the key themes regarding men and women...with words regarding men and women in the light of the Good News of Jesus Christ. Our emphasis on God's grace keeps reminding us...there is no Biblical reason for any one group of people claiming superiority over another group of people'.

[22] Meeks, 167.

[23] William Loader, 'Social Justice and Gender,' *Open Theology*, 6, (2020), 'Thus, the common human experience and the common male assumption found its secondary underpinning for the first century Jews, including Christ's followers, in Scripture itself. Men and women are seen positively as the work of the creator, including their positions in creation, i.e. men to rule creation and women not equal with men but nevertheless valued and respected', 2; 'Male fallacious reasoning about women's inferiority informed the assumption that the normal place for women was not in

public discourse and leadership. This flawed logic was the determinant for New Testament writers, their communities and wider society . The many exceptions in the beginning, around Jesus and the early decades are memories, like the women who followed Jesus to his death (Mark 15:40-41), the Samaritan with whom Jesus conversed in public (Johns 4:4-42, esp. 4:27), the 'sinners' at tax collectors parties (Mark 2:15-16; Matthew 11:19//Luke 7:34; Luke 15:1-2; 19:10) and the women at the empty tomb (Matthew 28:1-10; Luke 24:1-9; John 20:1-18). Luke's ideal of women performing supporting roles (8:2-3; Acts 9:36) allows, indeed encourages, room for them like Mary also to sit and (perhaps only) listen (Luke 10: 38-42), 3; 'If our faith allows us, it is better to take Scripture seriously, as we should on what it says about women and circumcision, and recognise that its truth also inspires us to deal with new situations and new knowledge in ways consistent with its core values of social justice. There will be howls of protest, just as there were against setting circumcision aside, but we will, to my mind, stand in better continuity with Paul and ultimately Jesus in doing so', 6.

[24] Scroggs, 308.
[25] Caird, 274.
[26] Pagels, 545.
[27] Caird, 273.
[28] Kirster Stendahl, *The Bible and the Role of Women*, trans. Emilie T Sander (Philadelphia: Fortress Press, 1966) 33; P K Jewett, *Man as Male and Female – A Study in Sexual Relationships from a Theological Point of View* (Grand Rapids: Eerdmans, 1975) 139; H Conzelmann, *First Corinthians* trans. J Leitch (Philadelphia: Fortress Press, 1975) 127.
[29] K Hopkins, *Conquerors and Slaves, Sociological Studies in Roman History* (Cambridge University Press, 1978) 122; Williams, 36; Adela Yarbro Collins, 'No Longer 'Male nor Female,' *JEAC* 1 (2019), 30: 'The phrase 'there is no longer slave nor free,' suggests that the legally enslaved person and the legally free person are one in their dependence on Christ.'
[30] *J Woolman's Journal* (Oxford, 1971).
[31] Stendahl, *Role*, 34; Jewett, 11.
[32] Collins Adela Yarbro. 'No Longer Male and Female,' 29.
[33] Jewett, 119; G Tavard, *Woman in Christian Tradition*, 17ff.
[34] Jewett, 143.
[35] Hans Betz, *Galatians*, 184 'One may venture the suggestion that Paul has lifted Galatians 3:26-29, in part or as a whole, from a pre-Pauline liturgical

context. In the liturgy the saying would communicate information to the newly initiated, telling them of their eschatological status before God in anticipation of the Last Judgment and also informing them, how this status affects, and in fact, changes their social, cultural and religious self-understanding, as well as their responsibility in the here and now'; 189 'The verse (28) contains three parallel statements in the present tense which define the religious, cultural and social consequences of the Christian baptismal initiation. The three statements... name the old status of the baptised and declare this old status is abolished. By implication a new status is claimed but no further explanation is given as this point. It is significant that Paul makes these statements not as utopian ideals or as ethical demands but as accomplished facts'; 190 'There can be no doubt that Paul's statements have social and political implications of even revolutionary dimensions... being rescued from the present evil aeon (Gal.1:4) and being changed to a new creation implies radical social political changes...'

[36] J. Otwell, *And Sarah Laughed, The Status of Women in the Old Testament*.

[37] Vern Bullough, *The Subordinate Sex* 40-49; L M Epstein, *Sex Laws and Customs in Judaism* (New York: KTAV, 1967); J Jeremias, *Jerusalem in the Time of Jesus* 359-60; L Swidler, *Women in Judaism, The Status of Women in Formative Judaism* (Metuchen, NJ: Scarecrow Press, 1976); G Shulman, 'View from the Back of the Synagogue, Women in Judaism', in *Sexist Religion and Women in the Church* ed. A Hageman (New York: Associated Press, 1974); Roland de Vaux, *Ancient Israel* 19-41; Jewett, 86-94; Meeks, 165-97; Scroggs, 289-91; Hull, 8-12; Mary Rose D'Angelo, 'Women in the Earliest Church: Reflections on the Problematique of Christ and Culture,' in *Women Priests*, 191-201.

[38] Crüsemann, 30 'As David Balch has shown, Josephus and Philo draw primarily on the ethics of Aristotle when they frequently and clearly support the subordination of women under their husbands, appealing to Scripture to justify this. An example is Josephus in *Apion* 2.201: 'He says that a woman is less than a man in every respect. This is why she should obey, not for the sake of her humiliation, but in order that she may be ruled. For God has entrusted power to the man'.

[39] Meeks, 170.

[40] Phylis Trible, 'Depatriarchalizing in Biblical Interpretation,' *Journal of the American Academy of Religion* 41 (March 1973).

[41] Caird, 274.

[42] James Dunn, *Jesus and the Spirit* (London: SCM Press, 1975) 308ff.

43 R Scroggs, *Paul for a New Day* (Philadelphia: Fortress Press, 1977) 1.
44 'Women and Priestly Ministry, The New Testament Evidence,' in *The Catholic Biblical Quarterly* 41 (October, 1979) 609.
45 Fiorenza, 154.
46 Bernadette Brooten, 'Junia ...Outstanding among the Apostles' Romans 16:7,' *Women Priests*, 141-44.
47 Elizabeth Schüssler Fiorenza, 'The Apostleship of Women in Earliest Christianity,' *Women Priests*, 135-1; Lynn H Cohick, *Women in the World of the Earliest Christians* (Grand Rapids: Baker Academic, 2009) 216 'After analysing the necessary literary and epigraphic evidence, it becomes clear that the male name Junias is unattested in the Greco-Roman world, while the female name Junia is widely witnessed. The pressing question becomes, why have so many of the Greek critical editions, and translations relying upon them, insisted on Junias? The answer lies in the committees' convictions that a female apostle was unlikely, and so this name Junias – unknown throughout the Greco-Roman world – was created ex nihilo to match their presuppositions.'
48 Fiorenza, 'Women'155.
49 Fiorenza 156-7; J M Ford, 'Biblical Materials Relevant to Ordination of Women,' *Journal of Ecumenical Studies*, 10 (1973) 670-8.
50 H G Liddell and R Scott, *A Greek English Dictionary*, New Edition Revised and Enlarged by Sir Henry Jones and Robert McKenzie (Oxford, 1966), 1526-7; *Stephanus Thesaurus Graecae Linquae* (1954), 7: 2003.
51 Lynn H Cohick, *Women in the World of the Earliest Christians*, 190 'Lydia is portrayed as a benefactor, a very privileged position in the Hellenistic world (including Judaism). We must not downplay her role in terms of our twenty-first century culture and imagine she cooked and cleaned for them. By giving them a place to stay, she revealed her generosity, and was thus honoured by the group. Another female benefactor, Phoebe, was also a deacon (Rom. 16:1-3) in the church at Cenchreae, a port of Corinth. Leadership and benefaction went hand in hand in the Greco-Roman world....Lydia was probably the leader of the group that continued to meet in her home...Presumably, Lydia followed the pattern found throughout the New Testament that the owner of the house in which the church met was also a church leader.'
52 In the ministry of Christ the role of women in exercising important aspects of ministry can be clearly seen. Thus, Peter Lockwood in 'The Woman at

the Well: Does the Traditional Reading Still Hold Water?' presents strong evidence, 12 'If apostleship is the first and foremost office in the early church (1 Cor. 12:28; Eph. 4:11), Mary of Magdala is arguably the person with the best claim to the title. According to most NT scholars the two marks of an apostle were 'having seen the risen Lord Jesus and having been sent to proclaim him (Brown 1975:692). Mary Magdalene is the one to whom the risen Lord first appears... and she is the first one commissioned to proclaim the good news of the resurrection – to the apostles themselves (John 20:1-18) ...; 23 'It is frequently argued that the public ministry should be reserved for males because Jesus called only men to be his disciples. It is worth noting in John's gospel how faintly the line of demarcation is drawn between the band of Twelve and the wider circle called to follow Jesus. Jesus prayed for those who would come to faith through the word of the apostles (17:20), but there is only one person – the Samaritan woman – through whose word a group of people is actually said to come to faith (4:39). John appears to be intimating that the Twelve and all who proclaim the name of Jesus and spread the gospel are co-extensive... No-one disputes that women were included in the wider circle of Jesus disciples. Mary sat at Jesus' feet (Luke 10:39), the posture of a disciple, and in his account of the crucifixion Mark speaks about the women, who used to 'follow' Jesus during his earthly ministry. 'looking from a distance' (15:40). A discipleship of women was unheard of previously and represents a remarkable elevation in their status. But the disciples of Jesus were never only disciples. Their tuition was only preparation. Discipleship led to commissioning to bear witness (or evangelism), delightfully encapsulated in the story of the Samaritan woman. She was instructed in the word of God. In fact, she was taught by the Word of God himself. And then she was sent to bear witness to that word of life.... The Lord issued no mandate for the ordination of women. But women were involved in the first rank of service to Jesus at the time of his earthly ministry. Therefore it is reasonable to conclude that no lesser role should be open to them today.'

[53] William Loader, 'Social Justice and Gender,' 2-3.
[54] CTICR, 21 March 2018, 3.
[55] Adela Yarbro Collins, 'No Longer 'Male nor Female' (Gal. 3:28),' *JEAC* 1 (2019), 35 '...by being baptised and 'putting on Christ', the members of the community voluntarily take on a new obligation'; 37 'It strongly suggests that all baptised persons are qualified to be full members of the church

and that no group defined by gender, ethnicity, social or legal status may be excluded from any type of service in the church. This reading implies, for example, that it is wrong for church authorities to deny ordination to women on the grounds of gender.'

[56] Karen B Neutel, 'Women's Silence and Jewish Influence: The Problematic Origins of the Conjectural Emendation on 1 Cor. 14:34b-35,' New Testament Studies, 65 (2019) 477 'The authenticity of the passage about women's silence in 1 Cor. 14 is one of the most hotly debated text-critical issues in Pauline scholarship. Did Paul's letter include the lines 'As in all the churches of the saints... for it is shameful for a woman to speak in church' or were these words added by a later hand?'; William Loader, *The New Testament on Sexuality*, 383, describes these verses as 'one of the most contested passages in Paul's undisputed letters ...Many combine the evidence of textual uncertainty with what they see as more substantial indications that the passage, or, at least, 34-35, is not original. Fundamental to such concerns is the contrast between Paul's acceptance of women's leadership roles in worship in 11:5, and generally as co-workers, and his silencing of women here. In addition, the appeal to the Law is seen as uncharacteristic'; Peter Lockwood, 'Does 1 Cor.14:34-35 Exclude Women from the Pastoral Office?' 32 'The most compelling way of accounting for the problem raised by 1 Corinthians 14:34-35 is that the regulation does not come from Paul's hand at all'. A discussion of this issue is outside the scope of this writing. Those who maintain the use of this text in the Theses of Agreement to exclude women from the ministry of the church are unlikely to cease their use of this text even if it would be irrefutably proved to be non-Pauline.

[57] *Lutheran Church of Australia*, 'A Theological Basis for the Ordination of Women and Men,' Approved for Release by the General Church Council, April, 2018.

[58] Cf. 1 Corinthians 14:3,4,12,19,23,26,28,33,40.

[59] Cf. Paul Jewett, *Man as Male and Female*, 114; S. Safari and M. Stern eds. In cooperation with D. Flusser and W.C. van Unnik, *The Jewish People in the First Century*, 920-1 '..women took no active part in the conduct of divine service' (i.e. in the synagogue) either as officiants or as readers of Scripture. This is clear from a halakah which runs 'All may come forward to make up the quorum of seven, even women and minors. But the sages say that a woman should not read the Scriptures out of respect for the congregation.'

End notes

[60] J.T.E. Renner, 'The Question of the Ordination of Women,' May 1974, unpublished, 4.

[61] See pp. 67-73

[62] Robert J. Karris, 'The Background and Significance of the Polemic of the Pastoral Letters,' 549-564; A. Lamaire, 'Pastoral Epistles: Redaction and Theology,' 24-41; T.A. Hanson, *Studies in the Pastoral Epistles* (London: Allanson, 1968); J Massingberd Ford, 'A Note on the Proto-Montanism in the Pastoral Epistles,' 338-346.

[63] *Luther's Works*, American Edition, (Philadelphia: Muhlenburg, (1960) 35: 170. The quotation is from Russell Prohl, *Women in the Church* (Grand Rapids: Eerdmans, 1957), 18.

[64] *Lutheran Church of Australia*, General Synod, 1968.

[65] 'Constitutions for Congregations,' *Lutheran Church of Australia*, (Tanunda, S.A.: Aurichts Printing Office, 1973), p.4.

[66] Ibid., p.6.

[67] Ibid., p.8.

[68] *Theses of Agreement*, 'Theses on the Office of the Ministry,' Doctrinal Statements and Theological Opinions of the Lutheran Church of Australia (Adelaide: Lutheran Publishing House, 1980) A 13.

[69] Andre Lemaire, 'Pastoral Epistles; Redaction and Theology,' 24 'No serious approach to the Pastorals can be imagined without facing the problem of their author'. Lemaire quotes Fr. Ceslas Spicq *Les Epitres Pastorales* (Paris: Gabalda, 1969) 'It is not without reason that the authenticity of the Pastorals has been either doubted or rejected from the beginning of the 19th century'.

[70] M. Dibelius and H. Conzelmann, *The Pastoral Epistles*, 1 'Literary dependence of Ignatius and Polycarp cannot be proven. The Pastorals are absent from the canon in Marcion.... 46 'Tatian rejected 1 and 2 Timothy, but not Titus. The letters are also absent in the Chester Beatty Papryi'.

[71] For a discussion of the authenticity, see Bruce Metzger, 'Literary Forgeries and Canonical Pseudepigrapha,' 1-24; Lemaire 27; Donald Guthrie *New Testament Introduction*, 675-683.

[72] Robert J. Karris, 'The Background and Significance of the Polemic of the Pastoral Epistles,' 549-564; T.A.Hanson, *The Pastoral Epistles*, 3.

[73] J.N.D. Kelly, *The Pastoral Epistles*, 6ff has shown that it is possible to fit the Pastorals into the historical data concerning Paul supplied in the Acts of the Apostles. Others dispute this. What appears obvious is that the Pastorals are addressed to a church situation where there is great concern for formal

structure of ministry and a heavy stress on tradition. Whether there could have been this development within the lifetime of Paul is unlikely.

[74] Dibelius and Conzelmann, 39-41.
[75] Ibid., 65-67
[76] J. Massynbaerde Ford, 'A Note on the Proto-Montanism in the Pastoral Epistles,' 338-346.
[77] Lemaire, 34-36.
[78] 1 Timothy 5:3ff; 3:11; Titus 2:3. Susan E. Hylen 'Women *diakonoi* and Gendered Norms of Leadership,' *JBL* 138 no 3 (2019) 687-702, argues that the ideals represented in the qualifications for *diakonoi* apply to women as well as to men.
[79] 1 Timothy 5:14; 2:15; Titus 2:4; 1 Timothy 4:3.
[80] 2 Timothy 3:6-7; 1 Timothy 5:11-15; 2:14-15.
[81] See above Chapter 3, 'The Corinthian Setting'.
[82] H.P. Hamann, 'The Problem of 1 Corinthians 14:35-35,' no date given, unpublished, p.2.
[83] See above Chapter 2.
[84] In addition to the articles quoted elsewhere, see also the commentaries of G. Holtz, *Die Pastoralbriefe* (Berlin, 1965) 72-73; A. T. Hanson, *Pastorals*, 36-37; Burton Scott Easton, *The Pastoral Epistles* (London: SCM, 1948); Dibelius and Conzelmann, *1 Corinthians*, 246.
[85] Dibelius and Conzelmann, 44 question whether the regulations for women 'really refer to the cultic behaviour. They rather comprise a general rule for women, here applied to prayer.'
[86] Cf. Mark 11:25; Matthew 5:23-24; 6:12.
[87] Dibelius and Conzelmann, 44.
[88] Kelly, 66.
[89] *Gynaikas* – the word used could be translated 'wives' and *andras* 'husbands.' Thus Luther, *Luther's Works* (St Louis: Concordia Publishing House, 1973) 28: 276.
[90] Cf. Luther, 273; *Calvin's Commentaries*: Ephesians – Jude (App. and A. Edition) 2177; Barratt 55; *The Interpreter's Bible*, (New York: Abingdon Press, 1955), 11, 404.
[91] 1 Peter 3:3-4; Dibelius and Conzelmann, 46.
[92] K.H. Rengsdorf, 'Didasko', G. Kittel and G. Friedrich, editors of T.D.N.T 2: 146f; James Dunn, *Unity and Diversity in the New Testament* 112, 130; J. Massengberg Ford, 'Biblical Material Relevant to Ordination,' 683

[93] Catherine Kroeger, 'Isn't it time for a new Look at 1 Timothy 2:12?' 6-7, unpublished paper.
[94] Hommes, 19.
[95] Prisca taught Apollos (Acts18:24-26); the four unmarried daughters of Phillip were involved in teaching through prophecy (Acts 21:9); see further, above. Lynn H Cohick, *Women in the World of the Earliest Christians* 223 'Judaism and Christianity were not exclusively or even predominantly male domains. Though he meant his comment disparagingly, Celsus might be closer to the mark than previously appreciated when he accepted the role of women (and slaves) in the church'.
[96] G. Delling, Hypotage, *Theological Dictionary of the New Testament*, 7: 46.
[97] *Hesychia* is found in 2 Thess. 3:12 with reference to 'some of you living in idleness, mere busybodies, not doing any work'.
[98] Kroeger, 4.
[99] Ford, 'Proto-Montanism,' 343.
[100] *The Pastoral Epistles*, 48; *The Apocryphal New Testament*, trans. M.R. James (Oxford: Clarendon Press, 1950), 280-1.
[101] Cf. *The Interpreter's Bible*, Vol. XI, 405.
[102] Cf. Lockwood, 'Five Pillars...' 33-46.
[103] Hanson, *Studies*, 47.
[104] Dibelius and Conzelmann, 46, note 15.
[105] Ibid., 47.
[106] Hanson, *Studies*, 66.
[107] Oscar Cullman, *The State in the New Testament* (London: SCM Press, 1963) 47.
[108] Lutheran Church of Australia, *Constituting Convention of the First General Synod*, 1966, Tanunda, South Australia.
[109] Commission on Theology and Inter-Church Relations, 'The Particular Question: May Women be Elected to Serve as (General) Synodsmen of a (General) Synod?' 1979: Mimeographed.
[110] It should be noted that that woman as mother was accorded status and honour, equivalent to man, in the Old Testament. Among the many useful studies on the role of women in the Old Testament, the following provide succinct summaries: Phyllis Bird: 'Images of Women in the Old Testament,' in *Religion and Sexism*, ed. Rosemary R. Reuther (New York: Simon and Schuster, 1974), 41-88; J.T.E. Renner, 'Woman in the Old Testament,' LTJ 9 (December 1975) 90-99; Leonard Swidler, *Women in Judaism: The Status of Women in Formative Judaism* (Metuchen New Jersey: Scarecrow Press, 1976).

[110] For an extended presentation and rejection of the arguments used by those who claim the creation and fall narratives of Genesis 2 and 3 establish subordination of woman and thus their disqualification from the ministry, see Peter Lockwood, 'Five Pillars that Totter and Crumble to Dust: Can Genesis 2 and 3 Support Subordination of Women?' *Interface* 8/2 2005: 32-47.

[111] Bird, 72

[112] For an extended discussion of humankind's creation in the divine image as an expression of his creation as male and female, see Paul K Jewett, *Man as Male and Female*.

[113] John A Bailey, 'Initiation and the Primal Woman in Gilgamesh and Genesis 2-3,' *Journal of Biblical Literature* 89 (June 1970) 143.

[114] Phyllys Trible, 'Depatriarchalizing in Biblical Interpretation,' 36.

[115] N P Bratsiotis ,' *'Ish – 'Ishashsh'* Theological Dictionary of the Old Testament, ed. G J Botterweck and H Ringgren, (Grand Rapids: Eerdmans Publishing Company, 1977) 1:227; 'Only after the appearance of *'ishshah* did he function as *'ish*;' Bird, 73.

[116] Bratsiotis, 226.

[117] U. Cassuto, *A Commentary on the Book of Genesis*, Part 1, 128.

[118] Douglas Judisch, 'Theses on Woman's Suffrage in the Church', *Concordia Theological Quarterly* 41 (July 1977) 38: 'Woman was created as an assistant (ezer) to man and by nature, therefore, possesses less authority than man... assisting man is her special role in the scheme of the universe.' P. Lockwood, 'Five Pillars...' 36f 'In English ears the word 'helper' conjures up someone to help with the household chores, an underling, even a paid employee. Nothing could be further from the truth. The word 'helper' (*ezer*) comes from the Hebrew word for protection, barrier or enclosure (*azarah*). Of the twenty-one occurrences of 'helper' in the Old Testament, fifteen are used of God (e.g., Ex.8:4; Deut.33:7,26,29). Given that the word 'helper' is used so often as a metaphor for God, or to portray the deeds of God, it is out of the question to suggest that the word could only imply a secondary or subservient status when applied to women.'

[119] Trible, 36.

[120] Trible, 37.

[121] Ibid.

[122] Bratsiotis, 226-7.

[123] Bird, 87, n. 89.

[124] My attention was drawn to this in correspondence from Victor Pfitzner.

End notes

[125] Eve is nowhere else referred to in the Hebrew Old Testament – except in Genesis 1-4, but note Tobit 8:6; Sirach 25:24; 2 Corinthians 11:3; 1 Timothy 2:13.
[126] Renner, 91.
[127] Trible, 40.
[128] Cassuto, 130; Wittwer, 24 'Galatians 3:28 assists us to recognise that patriarchy is part of the sinful distortion of God's creation. It is named as such in Genesis 3:16, where one of the descriptive phrases of the damaging effects of sin on human life is that 'he shall rule over you".
[129] Bird, 74.
[130] Trible, 41; H. Thielicke, *How the World Began*, 173 'The world has lost its peace because it has lost its peace with God'.
[131] Cf. Luther, 'Lectures on Genesis 1-5' *Luthers Works*, 1: 202-3; John Knox, 'The First Blast of the Trumpet,' *The Works of John Knox* ed. D. Laing 373.
[132] Jane Luecke, 'The Dominance Syndrome,' *The Christian Century*, (April 1977) 407.
[133] William E. Hull 'Woman in her Place: Biblical Perspectives,' *Review and Expositor*, Winter 1975) 15.
[134] See above Chapter 2.
[135] Hull, 17.
[136] Tanya Wittwer, 'The Authority of Scripture, Women's Ordination and the Lutheran Church of Australia,' *Journal of Lutheran Ethics*, Volume 9, Issue 12, (2009) 'We also believe that the authority of Scripture is best respected where the interpretation of Scripture is based on clear and consistent principles, interpretation is Christ-centred, and there is willingness to learn from modern scholarship. As we cannot be free of biases and choices we believe to know and state the assumptions we bring to the interpretive task is the position of greatest integrity'.
[137] Cf. Susan E Hylen, 'Women *diakonoi* and Gendered Leadership,' *JBL* 138, (2019) 687-702).
[138] 'A Theological Basis for the Ordination of Women and Men'; 'A Theological Basis for the Ordination of Women and Men: Background to the Draft Statements,' CTICR, LCA, 2018.
[139] See above Chapter 2, 'Females in Ministry in N.T. Times'.
[140] Herman Pech, 'Quoting Scripture on Social Issues – a Calculated Risk,' *The Way* 5 (July, 1980) 22.
[141] H. P. Hamann, 'The Problem of 1 Corinthians 14:34-35,' no date given, unpublished.

142 Marlen Crüsemann, 'Irredeemably Hostile to Women,' *JSNT*, 2000, 79, 20: 'A further example of the usefulness of 1 Cor. 14:34-35 (with 'divine inspiration and inerrancy and authority of the Holy Writ') for legitimating discrimination is found in Walter A. Maier, 'An Exegetical Study of 1 Corinthians 14:35b-38', CTM 55 (1991), 81-104. He writes, 'By the grace of God there has never been a woman pastor in the Lutheran Church- Missouri Synod'. 101.

143 See above Chapters 3 & 4.

144 Prepared by CTICR, approved for release by the General Church Council, 20 April, 2018.

145 General Pastors Conference 'Advice to the 19th General Convention of Synod' 2018.

146 'Ordination of Women and Men,' *Book of Reports*, Nineteenth General Convention of Synod, Rosehill, NSW, 2-7 October, 2018, 116.

147 J. Henderson, *Heartland eNews*, 14.11.2018. 'Post-convention Message to the Church' https://www.lca.org.au/category/lca-bishop/messages/

148 T. Hoffmann, 'My Trip to Germany,' *The News*, St Johns, Southgate, June 2019.

149 Anonymous, the responses of participants in my DMin thesis project were treated anonymously.

150 Statement prepared by Commission of Theology and Inter-church Relations, *Lutheran Church of Australia*, April, 2018.

151 J. Henderson, *Heartland eNews*, 14.11.2018. 'Post-Convention Message to the Church' https://www.lca.org.au/category/lca-bishop/messages/

152 J. Henderson, *Heartland eNews*, 27.2.2019. https://www.lca.org.au/category/lca-bishop/messages/

153 J. Henderson, *Heartland eNews*, 3.3.2020. 'Joint GCB CoB Meeting'. https://www/lca.org.au/category/lca-bishop/messages/

154 N C Schultz & C L Schultz, *The Key to Caring* (Melbourne: Longman Cheshire, 1990); C L Schultz & N C Schultz, *Caring for Family Caregivers: Group Leader Manual*,(1990). (Available from authors); *Care for Caring Parents*,(Melbourne: ACER Press, 1997); N C Schultz & C L Schultz,*Care for Caring Parents: Leader's Manual* (Melbourne: ACER Press, 1997); C L Schultz & N C Schultz, *The Caregiving Years* (Melbourne: ACER Press, 1998); E J Bruce & C L Schultz, *Nonfinite Loss and Grief: A Psychoeducational Approach* (Baltimore, MD: Paul H Brookes. Co-publishers: Sydney: Maclennan & Petty, 2001); *Through Loss* (Melbourne: ACER Press, 2004); N C Schultz, *Forgetting but not Forgotten: Understanding, Support and Spiritual Care for Persons with Dementia and*

End notes

Their Carers (Adelaide: Openbook, 2004); *A Life Reviewed – A Brief Account of My Life's Journey* (2014); C L Schultz, 'Family Caregivers of the Disabled in Australia' in D Modley, R Zanotti, P Poletti, & J Fitzpatrick, eds. *Home Care Nursing Services: International Lessons* (169-183), (New York: Springer, 1997); N C Schultz,' The Spiritual Dimension in Nursing Care' in C Rogers-Clark, K Martin-McDonald, & A McCarthy, eds. *Living with Illness: Psychosocial Challenges for Nursing* (160-170), (Sydney: Elsevier, 2004).

Selected Bibliography

Bailey, J. A. 'Initiation and the Primal Woman in Gilgamesh and Genesis 2-3,' *Journal of Biblical Literature* 89 (June 1970) 143-150

Barrett, C. K. *A Commentary on the 1st Epistle to the Corinthians* (New York: Harper and Row, 1968)

_____ The Pastoral Epistles The New Clarendon Bible (Oxford: Clarendon Press, 1963)

Beaton, Catherine. 'Does the Church Discriminate Against Women on the Basis of Their Sex?' *Critic* (June-July 1966) 21-27

Behr-Sigel, E. *The Ministry of Women in the Church* trans. Stephen Bigham Crestwood, (NY: St. Vladimir's Seminary Press, 1999)

Bendroth, M. L. & Brerton, V. L. eds. *Women in Twentieth Century Protestantism* (Champaign, Ill.: University of Illinois Press, 2002)

Betz, H. D. 'Spirit, Freedom and Law: Paul's Message to the Galatian Churches.' *Svensk Exegetitsch Arsbok* 39 (1974) 145-160

_____ Galatians (Philadelphia: Fortress Press, 1979)

Botterweck, G. and Ringgren, Helmer, eds. *Theological Dictionary of the Old Testament* Translated by John T. Willis. Revised Edition (Grand Rapids: William B. Eerdmans, 1977)

Boucher, M. 'Some Unexplored Parallels to 1 Corinthians 11:11-12 and Galatians 3:2 – The N.T. on the Role of Women' *Catholic Biblical Quarterly*, 31 (1969) 50-58

Brueggemann, H. C. 'The Public Ministry in the Apostolic Age,' *Concordia Theological Monthly* 22 (1951) 81-109

Brunner, Peter. 'Salvation and the Office of the Ministry,' *Lutheran Quarterly* 15 (1963) 99-117

_____ The Ministry and the Ministry of Women (St Louis: Concordia Publishing House, 1971)

Bullough, Vern. The Subordinate Sex (Chicago: University of Illinois Press, 1973)

Caird, G. D. 'Paul and Women's Liberty,' *Bulletin of John Rylands Library* 54 (Spring, 1972) 268-281

_____ Paul's Letters from Prison New Clarendon Bible (London: Oxford University Press, 1976)

Campenhausen, Hans von. *The Formation of the Christian Bible* Translated by John Baker (London: Adam Charles Black, 1972)

Carroll, Elizabeth. 'Women and Ministry,' *Journal of Theological Studies* 36 (1975) 660-687

Cassuto, U. *A Commentary on the Book of Genesis* Translated by Israel Abrahams. (Jerusalem: The Magnum Press, 1961)

Chaves, M. *Ordaining Women: Culture and Conflict in Religious Organisations* (Cambridge, MA: Harvard University Press, 1997)

Cohick, Lynn. *Women in the World of the Earliest Christians – Illuminating Ancient Ways of Life* (Grand Rapids: Baker Academic, 2009)

Collins, Adela Yarbro. 'No Longer Male and Female (Gal.3:28) Ethics and an Early Christian Baptismal Formula,' *Journal of Ethics in Antiquity and Christianity* 1 (2019) 27-39

Commission on Theology and Inter-Church Relations 'A Theological Basis for the Ordination of Women and Men' (Prepared for the 2018 General Synod, Lutheran Church of Australia, 2018)

———— 'A Theological Basis for the Ordination of Women and Men: Background to the Draft Doctrinal Statement' (Prepared for the 2018 General Synod, Lutheran Church of Australia, 2018)

_____ 'A Theological Basis for Why the Ordination of Women and Men Need Not be Church Divisive' (Prepared for the 2018 General Synod, Lutheran Church of Australia, 2018)

Conzelmann, H. *First Corinthians* (Translated by J. Leitch. Philadelphia: Fortress Press, 1975)

Cooke, B. *Ministry of Word and Sacraments History and Theology* (Philadelphia: Fortress Press, 1976)

Cullman, Oscar. *The State in the New Testament* (London: SCM Press, 1963)

Culver, E. T. *Women in the World of Religion* (New York: Doubleday, 1967)

Crüsemann, Marlene. 'Irredeemably Hostile to Women: Anti-Jewish Elements in the Exegesis of the Dispute about Women's Right to Speak (1 Corinthians 14:34-35)', *JSNT* (2000) 19-36

Daly, Mary. *Beyond God the Father: Towards a Philosophy of Women's Liberation* (Boston: Beacon Press, 1973)

_____ *The Church and the Second Sex* (New York: Harper and Row, 1968)

Danielou, J. *The Ministry of Women in the Early Church* (London: Faith Press, 1961)

Davis, J. 'Some Reflections on Galatians 3:28,' *Journal of Evangelical Studies* 19 (1976) 201-208

Dibelius, Martin and Conzelmann, Hans. *The Pastoral Epistles* (Translated by Philip Buttolph and Adelo Yarbo. Philadelphia: Fortress Press, 1972)

Doctrinal Statements and Theological Opinions of the Lutheran Church of Australia. (Adelaide, S.A.: Lutheran Publishing House, 1980)

Drane, J. W. 'Tradition, Law and Ethics in Pauline Theology,' *Novum Testamentum* 16 (1974) 167-187

Duisman, Jo. 'Concluding Unscientific Postscript on Women in the Church,' *The Lutheran Witness*. (March 1968) 19, 21, 23

Dulles, A. *Models of the Church* (New York: Doubleday, 1974)

Dunn, J. D. G. *Unity and Diversity in the New Testament* (London: SCM Press, 1977)

_____Jesus and the Spirit (London: SCM Press, 1975)

Easton, Burton Scott. *The Pastoral Epistles* (London: SCM Press, 1948)

Ellis, E. Earle. 'Paul and His Co-Workers' *New Testament Studies* 17 (1970-71) 437-453

Elert, Werner. *The Structure of Lutheranism* Translated by S. A. Hansen (St Louis: Concordia Publishing House, 1962)

Epstein, L. M. *Sex Laws and Judaism* (New York: KIAV, 1967)

Selected Bibliography

Faculty of Christ Seminary. 'For the Ordination of Women,' *Currents in Theology and Mission* 6 (1979) 132-143. (Now the Theological Journal of the Lutheran School of Theology, Chicago and Wartburg Theological Seminary)

Falconer, R. '1 Timothy 2:14-15 Interpretive Notes,' *Journal of Biblical Literature* 60 (1941) 375-370

Farmer, W. R., Moule, C. F. D. and Niebuhr, R. F. eds. *Christian History and Interpretation: Studies Presented to John Knox* (Cambridge: University Press, 1967)

Fiore, Benjamin. *The Pastoral Epistles: First Timothy, Second Timothy, Titus* SP 12 (Collegeville: Liturgical, 2007)

Fischer, Robert H. 'Another Look at Luther's Doctrine of the Ministry,' *Lutheran Quarterly* 18 (1966) 260-271

Fitzmyer, J. A. 'Authority on Her Head: An Examination of 1 Corinthians 11:10,' *New Testament Studies* 4 (1963-64) 410-416

Fraser, David and Eloise. 'A Biblical View of Women! Demythologising Sexegesis,' *Theology, News, and Notes* 24 (June 1975) 14-18

Fremsdorf, Wesley. 'Holy Orders and Ministry. Some Reflections,' *Anglican Theological Review* 59 (1977) 279-294

Gerhardt, Marjorie, *Women in the Ordained Ministry* A Report to the Division for Professional Leadership. Lutheran Church in America. No year given

Gerrish, B. A. 'Priesthood and Ministry in the Theology of Luther,' *Church History* 34 (1965) 404-422

Giles, Kevin. *Women and Their Ministry* (Melbourne: Dove, 1977)

———— 'The Ordination of Women: A Plea for a Fair Go,' in *Deliver Us from Eve* Edited by Barbara Thiering (1977) 41-52

———— *What the Bible Actually Teaches on Women* (Eugene: Cascade, 2018)

Goppelt, Leonard. 'The Ministry in the Lutheran Confessions and in the New Testament,' *Lutheran World* 11 (1964) 409-426

Goulbourne, R. M. B.*Reinventing the Wheel: Women and Ministry in English Baptist Life* (Oxford: Whitley, 1997)

Graebner, A. *After Eve: The New Feminism* (Minneapolis: Augsburg Publishing House, 1972)

Grant, R. *The Formation of the New Testament* (New York: Harper & Row, 1965)

Grelot, P. *Man and Wife in Scripture* (London: Burns and Oats, 1964)

Gryson, R. *The Ministry of Women in the Early Church* Translated by L. Laporte and M. Hall (Collegeville, Minn.: Liturgical Press, 1976)

Guelich R. ed. *Unity and Diversity in N.T. Theology. Essays in Honour of G. Ladd* (Grand Rapids: Eerdman, 1978)

Gunther, J. J. *St Paul's Opponents and Their Background* (Leiden: E. J. Brill, 1973)

Gyarmathy-Amherd, Catherine. 'The Ordination of Women in the Roman Catholic Church.' in I. Jones, J. Wootton, K. Thorpe eds. *Women and Ordination in Christian Churches International Perspectives* (London: T. & T. Clark, 2008)

Hageman, A. ed. *Sexist Religion and Women in the Church* (New York: Association Press, 1974)

Hamann, Henry P. 'The New Testament and the Ordination of Women' *Lutheran Theological Journal* 9 (December 1975) 100-108

———— 'The Problem of 1 Corinthians 14:33-35', No date given, unpublished

Hansen, Bruce. *All of you are One – The Social Vision of Galatians 3:28, 1 Corinthians 12:13 and Colossians 3:11* (London: T. & T. Clark, 2010)

Hanson, Anthony. *Studies in the Pastoral Epistles* (London: SPCK, 1968)

———— *Studies in Paul's Techniques and Theology* (London SPCK, 1974)

———— *The Pastoral Epistles* (Cambridge University Press, 1966)

Hardesty, Nancy. 'Evangelical Perspectives on Woman's Role and Status,' *Reformed Journal* (July-August 1973) 4-9

Harkness, G. *Women in Church and Society* (Nashville: Abingdon Press, 1972)

Henderson, John. 'Post-Convention Message to the Church' *Heartland eNews* (14.11.2018)

_____ *Heartland eNews* (27.2.2019)

_____ 'Joint GCG CoB Meeting' *Heartland eNews* (3.3.2020)

Hewitt, E., and Hiatt, S. *Women Priests* (New York: Seabury, 1973)

Holst, G. *Die Pastoralbriefe* (Berlin, 1965)

Hoffmann, T. 'My Trip to Germany,' *The News* (St. Johns, Southgate, June 2019)

Hommes, N.J. 'Let Women Be Silent in Church,' *Calvin Theological Journal* 4 (1969) 18-20

Hopkins, K. *Conquerors and Slaves* (Cambridge University Press, 1978)

Hull, W. E. 'Woman in Her Place: Biblical Perspectives,' *Review and Expositor* 72 (Winter 1975) 5-17

Hulme, William. *Two Ways of Caring* (Minneapolis: Augsburg Publishing House, 1973)

Hummel, Horace. 'The Holy Ministry from Biblical Perspectives,' *Lutheran Quarterly* 18 (1966) 104-119

Hurd, J. *The Origin of 1 Corinthians* (London: SPCK, 1965)

Hurley, J. B. 'Did Paul Require Veils or the Silence of Women?' Westminster *Theological Journal* 35 (1972-3) 190-220

Hyldahl, Niels. *The Early History of Christianity* English Edition (Frankfurt am Main: Lang, 1997)

Hylen, Susan. 'Women Diakonoi and Gendered Norms of Leadership,' *JBL* 138, 3 (2019) 687-702

Jeremias, J. *Jerusalem in the Time of Jesus* (Philadelphia: Fortress Press, 1969)

Jewett, P. K. *Man as Male and Female. A Study in Sexual Relationships from the Theological Point of View* (Grand Rapids: Eerdmans, 1975)

Jones, I. *Women and Priesthood in the Church of England: Ten Years On* (London: Church House Publishing, 2004)

Jones, I., Thorpe, K., Wootton, J. eds. *Women and Ordination in the Christian Churches – International Perspectives* (London: T. & T. Clark, 2008)

Judisch, D. 'Theses on Woman's Suffrage in the Church,' *Concordia Theological Monthly* 41 (1977) 36-45

Justes, Emma J. 'Theological Reflections on the Role of Women in Church and Society,' *The Journal of Pastoral Care* 32 (March 1978) 42-54

Kahler, E. *Die Frau in den Paulinchen Briefen* (Frankfurt: Gotthelf, 1960)

Karris, R. J. 'The Background and Significance of the Polemic of the Pastoral Epistles,' *Journal of Biblical Literature* 92 (December 1973) 549-564

Käsemann, E. *Essays on New Testament Themes* (London: SCM, 1964)

_____ *New Testament Questions for Today* London: SCM, 1969)

Kelly, J. N. D. *The Pauline Epistles* (London: Adam and Charles Black, 1963)

Kittel, G and Friedrich, G., eds. *Theological Dictionary of the New Testament* Translated by Geoffrey Bromley (Grand Rapids: Eerdmans, 1964-1976)

Knight, G. 'The New Testament Teaching on the Role Relationship of Male and Female with Special Reference to Teaching/Ruling Functions in the Church,' *Journal of Psychology and Theology* 3 (Summer 1975) 216-225

Kroeger, Catherine. 'Isn't it time for a New Look at 1 Timothy 2:12?' Paper Prepared for the Twin Cities Presbytery, USA, no date given

Kung, Hans. *The Church* (New York: Sheed and Ward, 1967)

Kurzinger, Josef. 'Frau und Mann Nach 1 Kor. 11:1f,' *Bibliche Zeitschrift* 22 (1978) 270-275

Lampe, G. W. 'Church Tradition and the Ordination of Women,' *Expository Times* 76 (1964-5) 123-125

Lemaire, Andre. 'Pastoral Epistle: Redaction and Theology,' *Biblical Theology Bulletin* 2 (1972) 24-42

_____ 'The Ministries in the New Testament Recent Research,' *Biblical Theology Bulletin* 3 (1973) 133-166

Liddell, H. G. and Scott, R. *A Greek English Lexicon* (Oxford, 1966)

Lindars, B. and Borgen, P. 'The Place of the Old Testament in the Formation of the N.T. Theology,' *New Testament Studies* 23 (1976-7) 59-73

Lindbeck, George A. 'The Lutheran Doctrine of the Ministry, Catholic and Reformed,' *Theological Studies* 30 (December 1969) 588-612

Loader, William. 'Social Justice and Gender,' *Open Theology* 6 (2020) 1-8

_____ *The New Testament on Sexuality* (Grand Rapids: W.B. Eerdmans, 2012)

Lockwood, Peter. 'Does 1 Corinthians 14:34-35 Exclude Women from the Pastoral Office?' *LTJ*, 30 (1996) 30-38

_____ 'The Woman at the Well. Does the Traditional Reading Still Hold Water?' *LTJ* 36 (May 2002) 12-24

_____ 'Five Pillars that Totter and Crumble to Dust: Can Genesis 2 and 3 Support Subordination of Women?' *Interface* 8/2 (2005) 32-47

Longstaff, T. R. 'The Ordination of Women: A Biblical Perspective,' *Anglican Theological Review* 57 (1975) 316-327

Luecke, Jane Marie. 'The Dominance Syndrome,' *The Christian Century* (April 27, 1972) 405-7

Luther, Martin. *Church and Ministry, Luther's Works*. Edited by Helmut Lehman and Conrad Bergendorf. Vol 40. (Philadelphia: Muhlenburg Press, 1960)

_____*Lectures on Genesis 1-5. Luther's Works*. Edited by J. Pelikan. Vol 1. (St Louis: Concordia Publishing House, 1958)

_____*Word and Sacrament 1. Luther's Works*. Edited by E.T. Bachman. Vol 35. (Philadelphia: Muhlenburg Press. 1960)

Lutheran Church of Australia. Official Report of Constituting First General Synod, Tanunda, S.A., (1966)

_____Convention of the 2nd General Synod, Albury, NSW. (1968)

_____Convention of the 6th General Synod, Parramatta, N.S.W. (1978)

_____Convention of the 18th General Synod, Rochedale, Qld. (2015)

_____Convention of the 19th General Synod, Rosehill, NSW. (2018)

Martin, W. J. '1 Corinthians 11:2-16. An Interpretation,' in *Apostolic History and the Gospel* pp. 231-4. Edited by W. W. Gasque and W. J. Martin (Grand Rapids: Eerdmans, 1970)

Marxsen, Willi. *The New Testament as the Church's Book* Translated by James Mignard. (Philadelphia: Fortress Press, 1972)

Massynbaerde Ford, J. 'A Note on the Proto-Montanism in the Pastoral Epistles,' *New Testament Studies* 17 (1970-71) 338-346

_____ 'Biblical Material Relevant to the Ordination of Women,' *Journal of Ecumenical Studies* 10 (1973) 669-694

Meeks, Wayne. 'The Image of the Androgyne: Some Uses of the Symbol in Earliest Christianity,' *History of Religions* 13 (1974) 165-208

_____ 'In one body: The Unity of Mankind in Colossians and Ephesians,' In *God's Christ and His People. Studies in Honour of Nils Dahl, 209-221.* Edited by J. Jewell and W. Meeks. (University of Oslo, 1977)

Menoud, Philippe. *Jesus Christ and the Faith* Translated by E. Paul. (Pillsbury, Pen.: Pickwick Press, 1978)

Metzger, Bruce. 'Literary Forgeries and Canonical Pseudepigrapha,' *Journal of Biblical Literature* 91 (1972) 1-24

Moffatt, James. *The First Epistle of Paul to the Corinthians* (London: Hodder and Stoughton, 1947)

Mollenkott, V. R. *Women, Men, and the Bible* (Nashville: Abingdon, 1977)

Moltmann-Wendel, Elizabeth. *Liberty, Equality, Sisterhood: On the Emancipation of Women in Church and Society* (Philadelphia: Fortress Press, 1978)

Moulton, J. and Milligan G. *The Vocabulary of the New Testament* (London: Houghton & Stoughton, 1952)

Murphy-O'Connor, Jerome. 'The Non-Pauline Character of 1 Corinthians 11:2-16,' *Journal of Biblical Literature* 95 (1976) 615-621

Neutel, Karin B. 'Women's Silence and Jewish Influence: The Problematic Origins of the Conjectural Emendation on 1 Corinthians 14:33b-35,' *NTS* 65 (2019) 477-495

_____ *A Cosmopolitan Ideal – Paul's Declaration 'Neither Jew nor Greek, Neither Slave nor Free, Nor Male and Female' in the Context of First-Century Thought.* (London: Bloomsbury T. & T. Clark, 2015)

Niebuhr, H. R. *The Purpose of the Church and Its Ministry* (New York: Harper & Row, 1956)

Odenberg, Christina. 'The Ordination and Consecration of Women in Sweden' in I. Jones, J. Wootton, K. Thorpe eds. *Women and Ordination in the Christian Churches International Perspectives* (London: T. & T. Clark, 2008) 113-122

Selected Bibliography

Official Report of the Forty Third Convention of the Evangelical Lutheran Concordia Conference of New Zealand, Upper Moutere, (May 1954)

Otwell, J. *And Sarah Laughed: The Status of Women in the Old Testament* (Philadelphia: Westminster, 1977)

Pagels, E. 'Paul and Women: A Response to Recent Discussions,' *Journal of the American Academy of Religion* 42 (September 1974) 538-549

Parvey, C. F. 'Ordain Her, Ordain Her Not,' *Dialog* 8 (Summer 1969) 203-208

_____ *Ordination of Women in Ecumenical Perspective* (Geneva: WCC, 1980)

Paulsen, Anne. 'The Ministry and the Ministry of Women,' *Lutheran World* 7 (1960) 231-232

Pech, Herman. 'Quoting Scripture on Social Issues – A Calculated Risk,' *The Way* 5 (July 1980) 18-23

Pedersen, J. *Israel 1* (Oxford Press 1959)

Pelikan, Jaroslav. 'Eve or Mary,' *Christian Ministry* 2 (May 1971) 21-22

Pfitzner, Victor. 'General Priesthood and Ministry,' *LTJ* 3 (1971) 97-119

Plaut, W. Gunther Genesis. *The Torah. A Modern Commentary* (New York: Union of American Hebrew Congregations, 1974)

Preus, David, W. 'Striding Towards Justice and Equity,' *Lutheran Standard* (April 17, 1979) 36

Prohl, R. *Woman in the Church* (Grand Rapids: Eerdmans, 1957)

Rahner, K. *Servants of the Lord* (New York: Herder and Herder, 1968)

Reumann, John. 'What in the Scriptures Speak of the Ordination of Women?' *Concordia Theological Monthly* 44 (1973) 5-50

Renner, J. T. E. 'Women in the Old Testament,' *LTJ* 9 (1975) 70-75

Robbins, M. 'St. Paul and the Ministry of Women,' *Expository Times* 46 (1934-5) 185-188

Ruether, Rosemary. *Religion and Sexism* (New York: Simon and Schuster, 1974)

———— *New Woman, New Earth* (New York: Seabury, 1975)

———— 'Sexism and the Theology of Liberation,' *The Christian Century* 90 (December, 1973) 1224-1229

———— *Women of Spirit* (New York: Simon & Schuster, 1977)

Rupprecht, Arthur, A. 'Attitudes on Slavery Among the Church Fathers' in *New Dimension in New Testament Study*, 261-288. Edited by Richard Longenecker and Merrill Tenney. (Grand Rapids: Zondervan Publishing House, 1974)

Safrai, S., and Stern M., eds. *The Jewish People in the First Century* (Philadelphia: Fortress Press, 1976)

Selected Bibliography

Sanders, E. *Paul and Palestinian Judaism* (Philadelphia: Fortress Press, 1976)

Sasse, H. 'The Crisis of the Christian Ministry,' *LTJ* 2 (1968) 34-46

Schlink, Edmund. *Theology of the Lutheran Confessions* Translated by Paul Koehneke and Herbert Bowman. (Philadelphia: Muhlenberg Press. 1961)

Scholer, D. M. 'Galatians 3:28 and the Ministry of Women in the Church,' *Covenant Quarterly*, 56 (1998) 2-18

Schüssler Fiorenza, E. 'Woman in the Pre-Pauline and Pauline Churches,' *Union Seminary Theological Quarterly Review* 33 (Spring/Summer, 1978) 153-166

_____ 'Feminist Theology as a Critical Theology of Liberation,' *Theological Studies* 36 (1975) 605-626

_____ *In Memory of Her: A Feminist Theological Reconstruction of Christian Origins* (2nd ed.; London: SCM Press, 1995)

Schweizer, E. 'Traditional Ethical Patterns in the Pauline and Post-Pauline Letters and Their Development (Lists of Vices and House Tables),' in *Texts and Interpretation* 195-209, eds Ernest Best and R. M. Wilson. (Cambridge University Press, 1979)

Scroggs, R. *Paul for a New Day* (Philadelphia Press, 1977)

_____ 'Paul and the Eschatological Woman,' *Journal of the American Academy of Religion* 40 (1972) 283-303

_____ 'Paul and the Eschatological Woman Revisited,' *Journal of the American Academy of Religion* 42 (1974) 532-549

Sexism in the 1970s. Discrimination against Women A Report of the World Council of Churches, Consultation, West Berlin, 1974,(W.C.C. Geneva)

Stendahl, K. *The Bible and Role of Women* (Philadelphia: Fortress Press, 1966)

_____ *Paul Among Jews and Gentiles* (Philadelphia: Fortress Press, 1976)

_____ *The Force of Tradition: A Case Study of Women Priests in Sweden* (Philadelphia: Fortress Press, 1985)

Studies the Function of Doctrine and Theology in the Light of the Unity of the Church Lutheran Council in the U.S.A. (1978)

Summers, Anne. *Damned Whores and God's Police* (Melbourne: Penguin, 1975)

Swidler, L. *Women in Judaism: The Status of Women in Formative Judaism* (Metuchin: Scarecrow Press, 1976)

Swidler, L., & Swidler, A. *Women Priests* (New York: Paulist Press, 1977)

Tavard, G. *Woman in Christian Tradition* (London: Notre Dame, 1975)

_____ 'Sexist Language in Theology,' *Theological Studies* 36 (1976) 700-724

Te Selle, S. *Speaking in Parables. A Study in Metaphor and Theology* (Philadelphia: Fortress Press, 1975)

The Ministry of Women. A Report of the General Synod Commission on Doctrine General Synod Office Sydney, (1977)

Thielicke, H. *The Ethics of Sex* Translated by J. Doberstein. (New York: Harper & Row, 1964)

_____ *How the World Began*. Translated by J. Doberstein. (Philadelphia: Muhlenberg Press: 1961)

Thiering, Barbara. ed. *Deliver Us from Eve. Essays on Australian Women and Religion*. Australian Council of Churches N.S.W. (1977)

_____ *Created Second* (Adelaide: Griffin Press, 1973)

'Theses of Agreement,' Volume 1, *Doctrinal Statements and Theological Opinions, Lutheran Church of Australia*. https:www.lca.org.au/services-resources-training/

Thrall, M. 'The Ordination of Women to the Priesthood,' *Theology* 57 (1954) 330-335

Tiemeyer, R. *The Ordination of Women* (Minneapolis: Augsburg, 1970)

Tolmie, D. F. 'Research on the Letter to the Galatians: 2000-2010,' *Acta Theologica* 32 (1) (2012) 118-157

Torjesen, K. L. *When Women Were Priests: Women's Leadership in the Early Church and the Scandal of their Subordination in the Rise of Christianity* (San Francisco: HarperCollins, 1993)

Trible, P. 'Depatriarchalizing in Biblical Interpretation,' *Journal of the American Academy of Religion* 41 (March 1973) 30-48

Tulip, Marie. 'Women and the Kingdom,' *International Review of Missions* 69 (April 1980) 135-142

Van Vuuren, Nancy. *The Subversion of Women* (Philadelphia: Westminster Press, 1973)

De Vaux, Roland. *Ancient Israel* (New York: McGraw Hill, 1965)

Wahlberg, Rachel. *Jesus According to a Woman* (New York: Paulist Press, 1975)

Walker, W. O. '1 Corinthians 11:2-16 and Paul's Views Regarding Women,' *Journal of Biblical Literature* 94 (March 1975) 94-110

Waltke, Bruce K. '1 Corinthians 11:2-16 an Interpretation,' *Bibliotheca Sacra* 135 (January – March 1978) 44-57

Webber-Ham, Cindy. 'Sexual Equality According to Paul,' *Brethren Life and Thought* 22 (Summer 1977) 167-170

Westermann, C. ed. *Essays on Old Testament Interpretation* (London: SCM Press 1963)

Wilder, Amos. *Theopoetic Theology and the Religious Imagination* (Philadelphia: Fortress Press, 1963)

Williams, M. S. 'The Man/Woman Relationship in the New Testament' *Churchman* 91 (January 1977) 33-46

Wittwer, Tanya. 'The Authority of Scripture, Women's Ordination and the Lutheran Church of Australia,' *Journal of Lutheran Ethics* 9 December (2009)

_____ 'Subordination and Headship: A Case Study in Lutheran Hermeneutics', *LTJ* (May 2019) 22-38

'Women and Priestly Ministry: The New Testament Evidence,' *Catholic Biblical Quarterly* 41 (1979) 608-613

Woman Suffrage in the Church. A Report on the Commission of Theology and Church Relations (Lutheran Church Missouri Synod, 1969)

Wootton, J. *This is our Story: Women's Ministry in the Free Churches* (Peterborough: Epworth Press, 2007)

Worley, A. *A Gathering of Strangers* (Philadelphia: Westminster Press, 1976)

Young, Frances. 'Hermeneutical Questions: The Ordination of Women in the Light of Biblical and Patristic Typology' in A. Jones, J. Wootton, K. Thorpe eds. *Women and Ordination in Christian Churches. International Perspectives* (London: T. & T. Clark, 2008)

www.ingramcontent.com/pod-product-compliance
Lightning Source LLC
Chambersburg PA
CBHW010706020526
44107CB00082B/2694